GROWING
through
the *Storm*

D1477320

Sheila Malsam

ISBN 978-1-68570-736-1 (paperback)
ISBN 978-1-68570-737-8 (digital)

Christian Faith Publishing
832 Park Avenue
Meadville, PA 16335
www.christianfaithpublishing.com

Some names have been changed to protect their privacy.

Some events have not been included to protect individual's privacy.

Printed in the United States of America

I dedicate this book to my parents who've taught me what love is and how to parent lovingly; to my son and daughter who've given a love so true and helped me become the mom, grandmother, and woman I am; and to my husband who loves unconditionally.

The thief comes only to steal and kill and destroy; I have come that they may have life, and have it to the full.

—John 10:10 (NIV)

A Note from the Author

So often we think God doesn't hear us during our struggles when we cry out to Him. Like many, after praying and not getting a quick response, I mistakenly thought it was up to me to find my own solutions and answers to struggles I encountered that I thought God didn't care about. As a result of my ignorance, I replaced God and His power with solutions that I thought were answers.

Despite my frustration from experiencing let downs, I sensed a knowing within my spirit that there was more to life than what I was experiencing. Foolishly, however, I clung to attachments such as doubt, fear, worry, self-pity, blame, insecurity, and unworthiness that kept me from receiving the answers and blessings God had in store for me. The vicious cycle of believing there was more to life, but experiencing disappointment instead because of my ignorance, kept me trapped and miserable until I experienced the awakening of God's truth, goodness, and unfailing love.

Unfortunately, many of us are guilty of living the life that I used to live. We can end up living in regret, beating ourselves up or living with bitterness, and repeating our mistakes over and over. Perhaps you can relate. Perhaps you, as well, have been stumbling through life trying to find solutions to your struggles and clinging to negative attachments that keep you from experiencing the blessings God has in store for you. If so, my friend, it doesn't have to be this way. Like me, you can turn to Jesus, surrender your all to Him, and discover the amazing love and grace He has for you.

I didn't come to know my Lord, have a personal relationship with Him, or realize His goodness until I had nowhere to turn but to Him after struggling for years with the frustration of an ongoing battle in a marriage I didn't feel honored. While going through the storm of feeling rejected as a wife and trying to do on my own what couldn't be done, I blamed God, fell into a pit, and prayed to be rescued. After being rescued by the grace of God, I developed a passion to teach others the goodness of our Lord and felt called to share my testimony of finding hope in Jesus and developing a personal relationship with Him.

The awakening in my spirit began after I turned to my Lord during my storm and discovered truth through scripture and chose to replace lies I had believed with His promises. From my struggles, experiences, and awakening, came a story of determination, inspiration, and hope.

I invite you to take a journey with me by reading my story and trusting that you, too, can be made anew, strengthened, blessed, and be set free by the power of the Holy Spirit to *"do all things through Christ who strengthens me" (Philippians 4:13 NKJV).*

In sharing my story, it is my intent to help others who struggle with a situation similar to mine by teaching them of God's incredible love and goodness so they, too, will put their hope and trust in Jesus, develop a relationship with Him, and be blessed!

Growing through the Storm is a story of triumphs and lessons learned while feeling rejected and trying to find solutions to my unwanted circumstances. I tell how feeling rejected and on my own led to doubt, fear, worry, insecurity, blame, self-pity, and feelings of unworthiness. I share how God revealed Himself to me and how He used my pain to grow me stronger, wiser, and more confident of His amazing love, which led to my relationship with Christ Jesus Who made a way where there seemed to be no way. I also share how I grew in my walk with my Lord and found hope and strength in His love and promises. I embraced the pain and struggles I believed God allowed in my life to draw me closer to Him. I trusted my Lord with the dreams I believed He placed in my heart. All of this in turn led me to experience blessings not only for my sake, but for loved ones as well.

Growing through the Storm includes points to ponder at the end of each chapter with thought provoking questions and comments including scripture and prayer for personal reflection.

Blessings await you, too, dear one! As I look back on the work God has done in my heart and the hearts of my loved ones, I pray that my story will encourage you to turn to our Lord and embrace the disappointments and challenges you face today, as well as the suffering that accompanies it. I pray it infuses your heart to see the goodness of God and His almighty power to do what we cannot do, that you put your hope in Jesus, our Lord and Savior, and believe *"with God all things are possible,"* as promised in *Matthew 19:26 (KJV)* when asked according to His will in His name. This will surely grow you into who you will be tomorrow by challenging you to rise above your circumstances, to find treasure in your struggles, and to seek your true purpose in life. Be blessed, my friend, and be a blessing!

Introduction

I will instruct you and teach you in the way which you
should go; I will counsel you with my loving eye on you.

—Psalm 32:8 (NIV)

I drove home with a heavy heart that cold December day from my
mom and dad's home after baking Christmas cookies with them.
Unable to silence my mother's words, "Your father and I are hurting
to see you hurting," I reflected on a prayer I had been praying for
some time.

This would have been my fourth year celebrating Christmas
without Ryan, my husband of three and a half years who expressed
a change of heart the day after he pledged his love to me in the presence of our family and loved ones during our wedding ceremony.

Ryan's confession that he wasn't ready to commit to the promise
of our marriage came as a shock to me, for I believed I had found
my "happily ever after" in him and trusted his love to be true. I felt
betrayed and hurt that the man I had shared such bliss and joy with
during our courtship, appeared to have lost interest in our dream.

We used to count down the days until the weekends arrived
that we'd get to see each other again. We counted down the weekends that remained after our engagement where we had to part from
one another until our wedding day. We were confident our children
from our previous marriages would blend nicely into one family
and looked forward to being role models as stepparents to each other's children. We were passionate about wanting to teach others the
well-being of mind, body, and soul. All this seemed lost and hope
was nowhere to be found as I watched Ryan drive off to continue

living the lifestyle he was used to living… I didn't understand what may have frightened him.

After days of frustration and outbursts of anger, the Lord gently spoke to me, "This too will make you stronger."

Not wanting to go through the suffering, but knowing God is all-powerful, all-knowing, all-good, and true to His Word, I lifted my head and acknowledged the response I was given.

Believing in the power of prayer and that God wanted to save my marriage, I prayed Ryan would grow in love with me as his wife. I prayed also for patience, for I knew the test of my faith would require a time of waiting.

Waiting wasn't easy, but necessary for God's plan to unfold.

Days passed and turned into weeks…weeks turned into months. I missed my husband, the man I believed to be true to his word while we dated. I missed sharing our dreams and being a couple. I longed for his knock at my door, for him to hold me and assure me of his love like before. I longed for a phone call to hear his voice…to hear him share his heart.

As time continued to pass and I continued to wait, I praised the Lord for blessings I was undoubtedly thankful for: my relationship with God and trust that He can make all things possible, my relationship with my son, Eric, my daughter, Jenna, and my parents who all stood by me no matter the mistakes I made, and their love that held me through the storm.

Before I knew it, months had turned into years. Family and friends witnessed the weight from my struggle grow increasingly heavier. At times it seemed unbearable. Still, I clung to hope that God wanted to restore my marriage and believed He could make all things possible.

I covered my hurt and walked with my head held high to reassure loved ones that I was okay. I assured them of my confidence in the Lord that soon my struggle would be over and they would see I had reason for hope.

My parents were concerned. They questioned my decision to hang on because they saw the ongoing struggle in my situation as never ending if I didn't let go.

city. I enjoyed evening bike rides like I used to take, long walks in the pastures, and the peace and quiet the country offered. More and more I daydreamed of being married and raising a couple of children with values I had grown up with.

Brad moved back home as well and started farming with his parents. It seemed that work had become priority for him. I noticed also that he seemed far more outgoing than me. He enjoyed social activities with his friends and wanted to be involved with community events, while I was content to be home, enjoying an evening walk or quiet time by the pond to gather my thoughts.

Several months later, Brad and I discussed the possibility of getting married. I expressed, however, that I didn't feel special to him like I did from the start of our relationship. It seemed after we both moved home and had the opportunity to see each other more frequently, I had taken a back seat to his friends, work, and social activities. I didn't feel like the treasure I once felt like. I shared with Brad that I no longer felt cherished, but rather taken for granted. Brad assured me, though, that it was my imagination. He stated it was a busy time of the year and there was much to be done with tending to the crops and animals. He expressed also that downtime with friends was important to him. Hanging out with them while golfing, hunting, playing basketball, and watching football gave him a break from his busy schedule.

I knew planting and harvesting were indeed busy times for farmers and that downtime was important. I struggled, however, with the frequency of sharing my boyfriend with his friends and attending parties with him that were hosted by his friends and other couples from the community. Since Brad enjoyed social activity, he socialized at these events while I was reserved and sat quietly in a corner desperately wanting to leave.

Bothered because I felt that my feelings were dismissed by the one I believed I loved, I turned to my oldest sister, Janet, and asked how to know if I was in love. Her response, "If you have to ask, you're not," got me to wondering if what I thought was love wasn't love after all.

I then confided in my mom about something not feeling "right" between Brad and me. I complained that Brad enjoys being with his friends and that I felt left out, insignificant, and disconnected from him… It wasn't the relationship I dreamed of having. Mom knew me to be sensitive about what did and didn't feel "right" to me. She knew as well how particular and set in my ways I was about wanting things the way I believed they should be, that I didn't back down, and that I was a nonstop dreamer, with expectations of my wishes being granted. She cautioned me about having too high of expectations and dreaming too big. She warned also that I'd get my heart broken if things didn't turn out the way I planned and advised that sometimes it's best to make do with what we have. I didn't see reason to stop dreaming and wanting what my heart desired, for without a dream, I wasn't living.

> *Hope deferred makes the heart sick; but*
> *when dreams come true at last, there is life and joy.*
> *(Proverbs 13:12 TLB)*

My mom's advice, though I know she was only trying to protect me, didn't resonate with what I felt in my spirit. I believed God created us to love and be loved and that He provided. I believed it was God Who put the desire in my heart to feel valued, cherished, and honored by the man to whom I'd one day pledge my love. I simply wouldn't hear of settling for less than what I expected in a partner.

Not willing to settle, yet not wanting to let go of my boyfriend either, I prayed in hopes that Brad would show the love and care I was seeking.

As time passed, I noticed marriages that looked to me as though they were unfulfilling. I began to wonder if my mom was right about dreaming too big. I began to question if it was just me who believed relationships were supposed to be more than just so-so. I found myself doubting that God really cares about relationships.

I didn't want it to be. I didn't want to let go of my expectations that a marriage is meant to be enchanting…even magical. But maybe it was so. Maybe God had bigger concerns than happily married couples. Maybe He wanted me to be satisfied and make do with the relationship I had with Brad.

Unsure of what was truth and feeling less confident that God cared about my desire for a happy marriage, I gave more and more thought to the advice my mom had given. I so wanted to feel treasured and honored. *But what if my wish to be loved the way I wanted was nothing more than a make-believe fairy tale…something that would never come true?*

It was then that Brad proposed to me, one year and a half after we had been dating… I was left to make a decision.

Because of the uncertainty I felt about our love being true, I was hesitant to accept the proposal. I wanted assurance that Brad truly loved me. I expressed concern again about not feeling cherished the way I felt during the earlier stages of our relationship. Brad shared that a marriage is what a husband and wife choose to make it. He reassured me that we would be happy.

Wanting to believe what I was told and fearing I'd end up alone if I didn't settle for what I had, I said "Yes" to Brad's proposal and assured my heart that everything would be okay.

It wasn't until another couple of years later that we set our wedding date; we weren't financially prepared. I was in no hurry, though. I still had reservation about our relationship and was looking for a sign to follow through with marriage. Plus, I was content being at home on the farm with my parents.

Still receiving no sign, but having reservation about getting married simply because of how I perceived relationships should be, I set my mind on a future with Brad and indulged in the preparation of my wedding. I enjoyed designing my gown that my mom helped me sew. I enjoyed picking out flowers and invitations, to making mints and wedding kuchen for the reception.

With my wedding only weeks away, that "something's not right" feeling still lingered in my heart as did, "there's more to love than this." I had already gone to the priest who instructed Brad and me with marriage preparation and shared my concerns. It appeared to me that he saw no reason for worry, which led me to think my thoughts were rambling, and surely I was making a big deal out of nothing.

Trying to silence my unsettled heart, I focused on other things. For instance, what it would be like having my own home to clean and decorate and having my own children to care for. I visualized enjoying the breeze coming through the open windows in my home during the spring, summer, and fall, just like I enjoyed growing up. I pictured hanging laundry on the wash line, growing a garden, and cooking supper for Brad. Surely if I showed kindness toward my husband, he would love and care for me in return.

After daydreaming about the life I looked forward to, and enjoying springtime, which always lightened my spirit, I finished the final touches of my wedding and imagined wonderful things awaiting me!

The future belongs to those who believe in
the beauty of their dreams. (Eleanor Roosevelt)

My gown was complete and beautiful as I dreamed, with a flowing skirt and hand sewn sequins covering the fitted bodice and tightly fitted sleeves. The tuxes were delivered and the decorations in place.

My wedding day arrived. The sun shone through my bedroom window that spring morning. I sat up in bed thinking about the day ahead of me. I couldn't wait to be seen in my gown with my hair and makeup all done and hoped Brad would like what he saw. I was excited for our first dance together as husband and wife and looked forward to celebrating with our guests.

Then I noticed it…the silence in the house. Mom and Dad got started with chores without me; I suppose because it was my wedding day. The silence gave me an eerie, lonely feeling. I looked around my bedroom and realized I wouldn't wake every day to it anymore. Nor would I have the time at home with my mom and dad that I've had the past years.

Not wanting the sinking feeling to settle in my spirit and bring down my mood, I pushed myself to get out of bed to prepare for a new chapter in my life.

With the help of my sisters who assisted with my makeup and hair, jewelry, and wedding dress, I was all set! I felt like a princess ready to be presented to her guests.

I stood at the entrance of the door in my little hometown church with my parents and attendants. Family and friends filled the pews trimmed with flowers and bows. Brad stood at the altar, waiting to take me as his wife.

As I made my way down the aisle with both my mom and dad at my side, my sister's advice about being in love echoed repeatedly in my thoughts. The sinking feeling of "something's not right" returned. *What if my love wasn't true? What if I was making a mistake?* Tears welled up in my eyes. *What was I to do?* All the preparations were made and our guests were expecting a wedding.

Just then, it seemed a gentle voice whispered in my spirit, "You're going to get hurt." Not knowing what to do as our guests were waiting, I quickly responded, "I'll make him love me," and continued walking, thinking I could change Brad after we were married.

I fought back tears when I hugged my mom and dad upon reaching the altar and said, "I love you." I then took the hand of the man I desperately hoped would love and care for me the way I expected and proceeded with my wedding.

After spending the night of my wedding at a hotel in a nearby town with my husband, a new beginning indeed took place. The home I anticipated to have with Brad was shared with his parents on his family farm. I never minded that we couldn't afford a honeymoon, but sharing a house left me to feel less of a wife. Why my in-laws chose to stay living in the house with us rather than moving, as planned, to the one they purchased as theirs was unknown to me, and I must admit, frustrating and disheartening.

I missed home. I went from having security and routine with my family to work that seemed never-ending. And though I wanted privacy and a home for just Brad and me, I felt compassion for my mother and father-in-law as I'm sure it was difficult for them to leave behind what had been "home" to them for many years. Still, I prayed that the arrangement of living with my in-laws wouldn't last long.

Several months passed and summer arrived. The animals born in the spring had all been moved to the pasture. The crops had been planted and were growing. My mother- and father-in-law had made the adjustment of relocating to their new home in town, and I looked forward to a fresh start with my marriage and making our house a home for Brad and me.

I kept the house tidy and decorated with what little we had and tended to the gardening and yard work like I was used to doing with my sisters and Mom back home. I enjoyed making home-cooked meals for Brad and welcoming him when he arrived home. Brad worked long, hard hours as did I with my job in town and chores on the farm. I realized this was all part of married life, but when Brad's leisure time frequently seemed to be spent with friends instead of me, I grew angry. I felt insignificant. I wondered if it had been a mistake to get married. I scolded myself for neglecting the gut feeling I had about getting married and for not giving serious thought to the long-term effect on my decision to marry had my relationship not been what I hoped it would be. I also pondered on my mom's advice on expectations, thinking I should be content with what I had, but because my spirit desired peace and harmony, a feeling of dissatisfaction remained within.

Whether or not I liked it, even if it had been a mistake, I was responsible for living with the decision I made. I came from a family with parents who stood by their word and toughed out the hard times. With that being said, I believed it wasn't an option to walk away from a promise just because things hadn't gone the way I had planned.

I had a promise to keep. I buried hurt and disappointment by cleaning nonstop inside and outside my home in my spare time and spent the evenings Brad wasn't home with my mom and dad pretending to be happy. Though I believed I was expected to keep my promise and live with the decision I made, I was hesitant to believe that I was expecting too much in my marriage. I prayed through tears nobody saw, asking God for the marriage my heart longed for.

Perhaps you can relate. Perhaps you too have faced disappointment because something didn't work out the way you had hoped.

marriage fell deaf on His ears…or perhaps I was being punished for something I did in my past, but I didn't know what.

Wanting an explanation, I boldly went to God and asked, "Why are You doing this to me?"

To my surprise, a gentle voice from within whispered, "It's not Me. This is the choice you made."

At that moment, I recalled the voice I had heard within my spirit on the day of my wedding; I realized it was God who cautioned me not to marry.

Could that have been so? my mind wondered. *Could it have been that it wasn't God's plan for me to go through with my wedding?* It had felt like such a tug of war back then between what my heart felt and the advice of others. *How was I to know which was the truth? How was I to know the voice I believed I heard within was God speaking to me that day instead of just a voice in my head?* I thought for a moment about where I would have been had I listened to the voice of caution on my wedding day. I regretted my decision to follow through with my wedding, but only for a second, because I wouldn't trade what had come from my marriage, my son and the relationship I had with him, for anything.

Where do I go from here? I wondered, *What now if it was so that I made a mistake? Will God forgive me and give me another chance at true love? Will He bless my marriage anyway and make it all I believe it should be or will I have to make do with what I have?*

No response, but the words "Forgive me, Father, for I have sinned" echoed within my spirit.

> *The Lord our God is merciful and forgiving, even though we have rebelled against him. (Daniel 9:9 NIV)*

POINTS TO PONDER

Is God whispering something within your spirit?

Do you have a dream that you believe God has placed in your heart? If so, have you surrendered it to God or like me, are you saying

"Yes" to what God is responding with "No" and believing you are in control?

My friend, trust that our Lord knows what is best and be open to the promptings of His Holy Spirit as He guides you on your path.

Do you struggle to measure up in areas of your life and feel as though you're not "enough?"

Do you wonder if God hears your plea?

Perhaps you've given up on a dream because you feel insignificant or because you believe the lie that you need to settle where you are even though your heart tells you otherwise. Or perhaps you've made a mistake and you wonder if God will forgive you and still come through for you.

Dear one, God will place dreams in the depths of your heart. Along the way, you may make mistakes, but the mistakes you make are never a surprise to God. He loves you no matter what. He delights in lavishing you with more than you can imagine because He is all-knowing, loving, and powerful. Surrender to Him your every need and the desires of your heart, for nothing is too big or too small for God. His ear is open every moment of every day. He hears every word spoken, even the whispers of your heart.

May he give you the desire of your heart and
make all your plans succeed. (Psalm 20:4 NIV)

Prayer: Heavenly Father, thank You for Your unending love and grace. Thank You for the dreams You have placed upon my heart. Help me to be sensitive to Your still, small voice within my spirit and to act in obedience so the plans that You have for me will come to pass. Forgive me, please, for the times I have neglected the promptings of Your Holy Spirit and gone astray. Forgive me for the times I have doubted Your love. Please reveal Your mercy and help me to surrender my all to You, knowing I am worthy of all that You have in store for me. In Your holy name, I pray. Amen.

Chapter 2

ASK

Ask and it will be given to you; seek and you will find;
knock and the door will be opened to you.

—Matthew 7:7 (NIV)

I confessed to God that I didn't know what truth was back when I said, "I do" to the man I believed I could change. I prayed to be forgiven. I prayed to be freed from the bondage I created and prayed for a second chance at love.

During that night while asleep, I dreamed of lying next to a man whose love for me was true. The man lying next to me accepted me completely. I felt loved, safe, and secure in his arms. My spirit was with peace, for I felt trust in this man. I longed for a love like that. I longed for the peace and assurance that I felt with the man in my dream.

While praying the following morning, I asked God for the kind of love that I had in my dream. I then turned my prayer book over at the completion of my request and saw the face of the man in my dream. It was the face of Jesus.

I scowled with disappointment, "You? I don't want You! I want a real man to love me!"

I shared with my mom the hurt I had been feeling because of my failing marriage. I explained also to her the dream I had and complained whose face I saw after my prayer request. My mom, bless her for her understanding and love for Jesus, said, "Honey, Jesus is the answer to your prayer."

I didn't want to listen. I didn't see how God could fill the void in my heart. I was angry because He wouldn't just give me what I wanted; I thought for sure it was up to me to find what my heart was looking for on my own.

After thinking through my circumstance and realizing I wasn't willing to part from my son in exchange for the possibility of true love in a companion, it made sense that another child would fill the soon-to-be emptiness from Eric going off to kindergarten.

With those thoughts in mind, my plan was to have another baby.

Having believed I found the solution for filling the void to come, I shared my plan with my doctor to have another baby. My doctor's thoughts were different than mine. He recommended that I visit with a psychiatrist before making plans to have another baby.

I followed through with seeing the psychiatrist my doctor recommended. He diagnosed me with depression and advised that I not bring a baby into my marriage considering its condition. On a scale from one to ten, ten being severely depressed, the psychiatrist rated me a 9. The reason he rated me a 9, he said, and not a ten was because I didn't have suicidal thoughts. Such thoughts never crossed my mind, for I cared very much for the ones I would have left behind: my son and my parents, that is. Not being there for them wasn't an option… I had to fight to stay strong for my loved ones.

The psychiatrist sent me home with self-help CDs on thinking positively and suggested for me to show love toward Brad even if I didn't feel loved the way I expected, for in due time, we receive what we give. The discussions on the CDs inspired me to hope that my marriage would improve if I put forth the effort to keep a more positive frame of mind. I committed to taking the information on the CDs seriously for the sake of my well-being, my marriage, and my family. I wanted to feel a deeper appreciation for my husband.

After a couple of visits with the psychiatrist, it was recommended that Brad join me to hear what was on my heart. Brad joined me as requested and agreed during the session to make our marriage a priority. I was confident he was sincere and trusted he'd be mindful of my needs as his wife; I looked forward to a brighter tomorrow.

It was then that Brad took a job as a farm hand for a friend as finances had become a serious matter for us. Brad had the idea also to utilize the land we rented from his parents by starting up a hunting business for pheasants and waterfowl. I was reluctant at first; I doubted we'd find clients willing to pay to hunt, but agreed that his plan was worth giving a try.

We worked together as a team to prepare for the hunting operation. We built bunk beds and purchased mattresses, pillows, and blankets. My part was to plan a menu and prepare the meals that our clients would be served. It was a task I was qualified in doing with the experience I had preparing meals with my mom and sisters for our family of twelve on a daily basis. I was in charge of the cleaning as well. Brad's responsibility was to book the hunts and guide our clients on where to hunt. I enjoyed working with Brad toward a goal we shared.

The first hunting season arrived. I wasn't sure how I'd manage to get through it. I had been hurrying to get the last of the details completed the day before the season started and was still taking blankets off the wash line for fresh bedding as the hunters were piling in that Friday evening to get settled for their hunt.

The following morning, day one, I woke early to prepare breakfast for twenty-plus hunters. After washing the dishes, tidying up, and scrubbing the mud off the floor that got tracked in, it was time to begin preparing the evening meal. Before I knew it, the hunters were back from their hunt, had cleaned their birds, and were ready for supper. While they sat to eat, I dashed back and forth from the kitchen to the bedroom to get Eric and myself ready for church services that evening. I recall running out the door explaining that I'd be back after church to clean up from supper.

I wanted to crawl into bed when I got home from church and go to sleep; instead, I had a stack of dishes to wash, the floor to sweep, and the house to tidy again.

I escaped to the bathroom for a time out and sat on the floor.

"I'm tired, God…please help me through this," I prayed.

Come Monday, I thought, *things will only get tougher*. I'd have the hunters to cook and clean for, plus my daycare children back during the week to provide for. I didn't see how I was going to keep up with the responsibility. Knowing though, that the mess I had waiting for me at the time in the kitchen wouldn't go away on its own, I pulled myself up and got to cleaning again.

While Brad entertained our clients, I tidied up and prepared what I could for breakfast the next morning. From there, I went to Eric, who had been enjoying the attention from hunters. We said our prayers, read a story, and shared about our day.

Surprisingly, I made it through the rest of the season, and quite well I would say. There was always just enough time to get a room cleaned and prepare for the new group of hunters who were to arrive. It did help that Eric and the daycare children enjoyed the attention of the hunters. I took advantage of the moments the hunters entertained the children and hustled to fold towels and fix beds before they headed out for their hunt for the day. I even made time to continue volunteering at preschool. Fortunately, there was always a hunter Eric enjoyed the company of after the evening meal while I cleaned up the kitchen and dishes. Best of all, there was still time to cuddle Eric at the end of the day.

I realized the worrying I did over operating the hunting business while continuing my daycare was time wasted.

By the time hunting season was over, Eric had gotten to know several hunters he hoped would return to our house. I also looked forward to seeing many of them return. I gained self-esteem and confidence from praise and compliments the hunters gave for my hospitality, hard work, and home-cooked meals. I was appreciative of them, but also appreciative that they were gone so I could enjoy quieter evenings with just Eric and Brad.

Maybe you as well have spent unnecessary times worrying over something that ended up never happening the way you feared. I've lost track of the countless times I've been guilty of this. In the end, I gave thanks and praise to God for His act of faithfulness and developed a deeper trust in Him. Regretfully though, I've succumbed to my weakness and found myself worrying needlessly again after encountering a new crisis more often than I want to admit. Praise God, however, that He is good, knows we are all a work in progress, and continues to shower His children with His ever-lasting love.

> *For everyone has sinned; we all fall short of*
> *God's glorious standard. Yet God, in his grace, freely*
> *makes us right in his sight. (Romans 3:23–24 NLT)*

It seemed at this time, that everything was headed in the right direction. I liked that I felt a bond with Brad as we worked on a project together, it was successful and finances had finally improved.

I learned that Christmas that I was two months pregnant. I was excited about the pregnancy and hopeful that the positive connection Brad and I developed through our hunting business would remain.

As it turned out, it was a struggle getting through the holidays and the next month or so. I was tired and had little energy which made it difficult to be the mom I wanted for Eric. Plus, I was cautious about overdoing it so I wouldn't develop preterm labor and end up in the hospital like I did when I was pregnant with Eric. He needed me to take care of him.

It turned out that the connection between Brad and I didn't last the way I had hoped. Brad was outgoing, fun-loving, and enjoyed social activities. I came to the realization that I couldn't change who he was. I could only do for us what I had control over. I stayed in shape, presented myself well, and gave of my time. I didn't know what more I could do to be a better wife. I knew, however, that I had to be strong and take care of myself for the sake of my son and unborn child I was carrying.

Eric was a comfort and support during my pregnancy. He showed care for me when I didn't feel well by cuddling me on the couch when I needed a rest and concern by patting my shoulder when I hovered over the toilet. I loved his tender heart and compassion. The love and kindness he showed cheered my heart. It made me feel treasured, cherished, and significant. Though he was young, he was a safe-haven for my heart.

By spring, I had more energy and Eric and I got back to spending time outside, crafting projects, and baking treats like we enjoyed. My heart was in good spirits and I remained well without the risk of preterm labor. Praise God!

That summer, nine days after Eric's fifth birthday, a beautiful, bald-headed baby girl came into our lives early in the morning. Aside from being born with no hair on her head, my daughter resembled her brother.

While with my brother, Cory, and his family during the delivery of my daughter, Eric picked out an outfit for his sister with pink sandals to match. He smiled, looking so proud as he presented his gift and held his sister. There was no doubt he was going to be a good big brother. He was protective and mindful of others. I saw that not only in how he cared for me and one of the daycare children in particular that he looked out for, but also in how he cried for Tigger in *The Tigger Movie* when Rabbit told Tigger he couldn't bounce anymore. It took watching the movie several times with my son to discover what it was that moved his heart to tears. If Eric had a heart for characters in the movies, he was sure to have a heart for his sister and look after her.

After Eric and his dad left the hospital for home that evening, I rocked my daughter in my arms. While rocking her, she looked me right in the eyes, bright-eyed and wide awake as though she didn't want to miss a thing. My daughter had a look on her face as though she knew she had her mama's heart. It was true. Though I was exhausted from the morning delivery and no nap, I couldn't help falling for my baby girl that very moment...she was irresistible.

My daughter, who was given the name, Jenna, and I went home from the hospital the following day. I could tell Eric adored his sister by the look in his eyes as he held her. He was a good helper and enjoyed watching over Jenna by winding up her swing while I hung the laundry on the wash line, prepared a meal, tidied the house, or gathered vegetables from the garden. I wouldn't have been able to keep up with household chores and the yard and garden the way I did without the help of Eric as Brad was busy working in the field. I appreciated Eric's help and care for Jenna.

A month after coming home from the hospital, my daycare was back in operation as was preschool, which Eric and the daycare children still attended. It was also time to prepare for our second hunting season in which I knew I was in need of help because Jenna required much of my time.

Our neighbor, Pam, who was a friend of mine, was kind and offered to help by preparing breakfast and washing the dishes so I could tend to Jenna in the morning. Pam's help was much appreciated and made the season go smoothly.

As the second hunting season wound down, the Christmas season was upon us. What fun it was to bake Christmas cookies and decorate them with Eric and to shop for a present with him for his sister and his dad. I cherished family time and treasured cuddling with my children as we watched Christmas shows. I enjoyed looking at Christmas lights with them and their dad, celebrating with a special meal for us before church services on Christmas Eve, opening presents together when we arrived back home, and spending Christmas Day with our parents and siblings.

Family time is not a matter of convenience.
It's a matter of priority. (Author Unknown)

Spring sprang into season several months later and so did Jenna's determined "can do" spirit. At only nine months old at the time, she got up on her own from crawling and walked across the floor without help. From then on, she needed no assistance catching kittens on the farm! Her unwavering spirit at her young age amused me. She waited for no one's approval, unlike her brother who had a more cautious, softer, gentler side to him. I witnessed his compassionate, gentle spirit when he freed a turtle that he cared for a short time and was wanting to keep. When I pointed out to him that the turtle was without its home and family, there was no doubt he knew what needed to be done.

Time passed so quickly after having Eric and Jenna. When summer arrived, Eric turned six years old and Jenna was one already. Far sooner than I wanted, my children would be grown and on their own. I had already prematurely cried my share of tears over having to let go one day, even though it was another ten-plus years for that to happen.

Not wanting any regrets, I took every opportunity to spend time with my children. I held dear the memories I made enjoying long summer days with them, tucking them into bed at night, and getting to cuddle them in the morning. I especially gave myself to my children that summer as Eric was going to be starting kindergarten in the fall.

Riding the four-wheeler through fields and pastures, watching sunsets, digging in the sandbox, attending Eric's T-ball games, playing hide-and-seek until the first star appeared to make a wish, and reading stories in the tent was simple and carefree fun I treasured. There'll never come a day I'll regret time with my children, nor be a day that I won't want to spend time with them and their children.

I so did not want that summer to come to an end as I wasn't ready for Eric to be away at school. Prior to the first day of school, I cried every day those last few weeks, not wanting to let him go. Jenna would miss him too. She was used to following her brother wherever he went and having him by her side. That's one thing about growing up in the country. You grow close to your siblings because they are what you have.

> The bond that links your true family is not one of blood, but of respect and joy in each other's lives. (Richard Bach)

The day I had been dreading arrived—Eric's first day of school. Thankfully, he was excited. And thankfully, several of his daycare buddies were his classmates, all of whom were familiar with the school setting, thanks to having attended preschool.

While I drove Eric, along with Jenna, to school that morning, I felt an unpleasant knot in my stomach. I had been praying for strength for this day for a long time. I prayed until the moment we walked into Eric's classroom.

As we entered the classroom, we were greeted and welcomed by Eric's daycare buddies and his teacher, Ms. Wisk. My heart felt lighter already. Ms. Wisk came across as a truly kind and compassionate woman. Her gentleness and the enthusiasm I sensed in Eric brought comfort to my heart and peace to wish him and his teacher a good day.

After hugging Eric goodbye, I took Jenna's hand and we made our way to the exit before she got too comfortable in her brother's classroom. Sooner than I wanted, it would be her I'd be hugging goodbye. But at the time, she was mine to take home and enjoy our time together!

After she and I arrived back home with my niece, Jamie, who I was still babysitting, I began preparing for the third hunting season while the girls entertained each other. I was pretty organized by this time, but welcomed the continued help of my friend, Pam, during hunting season. Her help was a blessing since I had two children to care for, as well as homework and school projects Eric would need help with. It was also a blessing that Eric enjoyed school as much as he did. God was good to help all of us adjust to a new routine.

I enjoyed watching a cartoon with Eric while he ate breakfast before the school bus arrived. I looked forward to greeting him after school and hearing all about his day and what he learned. He was happy and that made me happy.

At the end of another hunting season, I enjoyed having more time with my children again. I looked forward to the days Eric had off from school so he could be home with Jenna and me. I held dear to my heart the little things like baking cookies, making crafts, and playing games with them. I especially remember connecting blankets to the bottom bunk of their bed at night to form a tent where we snuggled together. I cherished cuddling with them while we talked and read bedtime stories; my favorite being, *Love You Forever*, by Robert Munsch.

I hoped my children felt secure and safe in my presence just like I felt in my mom's presence. I wanted them to feel loved and appreciated like my mom made me feel. I loved my children's hugs and kisses and enjoyed massaging their backs until they drifted off to sleep. Even though my children grew quicker than I wanted, it was a journey I wouldn't have traded for anything, the most rewarding journey I had ever had.

> The love of a mother is the veil of a softer
> light between the heart and the heavenly Father.
> (Samuel Taylor Coleridge)

As much as I thrived on caring for my children, and feeling loved by them, my heart still desired a love that a husband and wife share. My heart longed to feel cherished like the times Brad wrote pretty love poems and sent cards to me while we dated. It wanted attention and affection, approval and praise, the kind of praise I received during the hunting season from clients who were appreciative of my hospitality and hard work.

One hunter in particular made me feel especially valued. Michael was a hunter like any other that I introduced myself to at the time of his arrival and then went about my work as usual. He was polite and offered his help like many of the hunters did, but went out of his way to offer a hand with extras, like emptying the trash and making the morning coffee while carrying on a conversation with me. He was jovial and fun to be around.

After the third season passed, I thought about Michael from time to time. Thoughts of how I felt in his presence put a smile on my face. I wondered what life was like back home for him. I thought about the way my heart felt lightened when he teased me about the pumpkin I carved with my children for Halloween (it looked nothing like the picture in the magazine). Michael's energy made me feel young and vibrant.

I longed to share those kinds of feelings with Brad. It seemed, though, we lacked common interests and the desire to put a smile on each other's face. I didn't know at that point in my life what to think of my marriage other than I had to make do with the decision I made by following through with my wedding vows. What I did know was nothing was more precious to me and constant than my children and parents. I may not have had the marriage I had hoped for, but I was blessed ten-fold with Eric and Jenna and the beautiful relationship I had with them and my parents. Accepting of what I didn't have in exchange for what I had been given was a small sacrifice that I believed was necessary for the well-being of my children.

> The greatest sacrifice is when you sacrifice
> your own happiness for the sake of someone else.
> (Author Unknown)

With Christmas right around the corner, I found joy in celebrating the season. What a delight it was to watch Eric sing his heart out in the program at school and in church. He had a smile that lit up any room. It was fun, too, that Jenna was of age to take a part in cookie decorating, enjoying Christmas shows like *Frosty the Snowman,* and opening presents. Truly, it was my heart's desire to experience occasions such as this and the innocence of my children's love. I remember the thoughtfulness of Eric decorating my birthday cake in the spring of that year with the help of his sister, and the card he made with a rainbow in the sky because I like rainbows. The smile on Eric's face when he presented his gift still brightens my heart. No matter the circumstance, I'll not take their love for granted...my children were the sunshine in my day, the joy in my soul, and the loves of my life.

Of course, my mom and dad were dear to me too. Even in my thirties, they were still a comfort for me. They welcomed my children and me at all times. We enjoyed Mom's home cooking and never left her and Dad's house without Dad giving us a treat from the candy jar. It was a tradition my dad's mom passed on to him. We also enjoyed fishing at the river with them and spending overnights at their cabin. Since fishing was an activity I enjoyed with my parents and siblings, it was an experience I wanted my children to have with my parents too.

We spent frequent visits with my sister, Mary, and her family as well, who lived on a farm close by ours and with my brother, Cory, and his family, who lived in town. Having a big family that lived nearby was great. There was always someone to visit and cousins that my children enjoyed.

At home, I enjoyed walking the tree grove near our yard with my children as we looked for wildlife and making homemade noodles while we sang and danced to Kidz Bop CDs. I enjoyed riding the four-wheeler with them at the end of the day in the summer, playing hide-and-seek, kickball, watching the sunset, and wishing on the first star every chance we had.

When I wished on a star, I wished for closeness forever with my children and family, and true love with my companion to be mine. I didn't just wish it; I prayed it throughout every day.

After making my wish one evening that summer, Eric, who had just turned seven years old, shared that he wishes the same wish as I did. Certain that he didn't know what I had been wishing, I wrapped my arms around his small frame and looked down at him about to say, "Oh, honey, if only you knew," and to my surprise, he said with a look of pure innocence in his eyes, "I wish true love for you too."

Taken back by the sincerity of my son's words, I stood in silence with him in my arms. It had always seemed to me that he was mature for his age and aware of what I was feeling without being told. It was like our souls were connected. *Could that be?* I wondered. *Could our souls be connected and in tune with one another or was it that Eric's soul was connected and in tune with God?* Whatever the answer, I was in awe of God's goodness and His blessing of the relationship with my son. Eric's character was that of a loving parent, calming and soothing to my soul. He accepted me for all that I was and brought peace and reassurance to my heart with his gentle and soothing spirit like the Man in my dream, Jesus.

I wondered, *Do all parents experience this or was what we shared unique?*

> Wisdom often comes from the mouth of babes. (George R. R. Martin)

Too soon, summer came to a close again. It was time for Eric to go back to school and time to start preparing for another hunting season.

Eric was off to a good start in the first grade, thanks to his experiences in kindergarten the previous year and to his aunt, my sister-in-law, Sandy, who he adored for his teacher. I looked forward to seeing the school bus come down the road at the same time after school every day, as did Jenna who watched from the window and yelled, "Brober coming!" as soon as she saw the bus. After greeting our golden retriever, Eric shared nonstop for several minutes what he did and learned in school. Seeing Eric happy brought smiles to my heart.

Jenna, two years old at that time, was a busybody while her brother was in school. She changed her outfits several times a day which Eric could never understand. "It's a girl thing," I'd tell him. She entertained Jamie, who I had still been babysitting, by giving her rides outside in the motorized jeep Eric had outgrown. Then she gathered the clothespin aprons my mom had sewn for her and Jamie and the doll clothes to hang them on the pretend wash line I strung in the living room. After tiring from that, Jenna found something else for Jamie and her to do.

Jenna had a creative imagination and unique style of her own in every aspect of life. She lacked patience, however, to do projects that lasted more than a couple of minutes, unlike her brother who could sit for at least an hour at a time driving his toy tractors through play dough we made or painting and rebuilding his toy trucks.

I found joy in watching Jenna and Jamie play while I got things ready for the upcoming hunting season while Eric was at school. As I prepared for another season, I gave thought to the previous year and wondered if Michael would be returning with his dad to hunt.

After a couple of weeks into the season and a busy day of greeting hunters, cooking, and cleaning, I was pleasantly surprised to notice a familiar truck drive into the yard and see Michael, who I secretly hoped would return, get out of his truck and make his way to the house. I trembled with excitement watching him pass by the other hunters to make his way to the door. I couldn't help the flutter in my heart when he arrived at the door and said I looked even prettier than the year before, though I looked a mess in just my blue jeans and t-shirt.

I grew fond of Michael that season. I was drawn to his fun-loving personality and enjoyed his attention, compliments, and help. He made me feel valued. He appreciated the simple things in life. One evening I asked what he looks at up in the sky every night.

"The stars," he replied. He shared that where he comes from the stars don't shine like they do in South Dakota. Michael told me I was fortunate to have two beautiful children to get to stay home with and to live out in the open where the stars shine brightly. He was right. Living in the country was something all right and my children were blessings I was thankful for indeed. Not every mom gets the opportunity to stay home with her children like I was able to.

> Don't take for granted the love this life gives you. (Tim McGraw)

I wondered if Brad noticed another man paying attention to me...if he did, he didn't show it. It didn't matter; my spirit felt fed and alive. Michael brought back the "me" that I used to be.

I didn't want the joy I found in the friend that I made that week to turn to just a memory. I wished the happiness Michael brought to my heart would have lasted forever. It couldn't though...he wasn't mine to keep, nor could I be his. Michael had a home where his daughter and business he owned waited, and I had a husband to be true to.

When it came time for Michael to go, I felt my heart breaking. I did my best not to let my emotions show as he and his dad packed up their belongings. "Thank you for coming," I said with a forced smile. "I sure enjoyed having you."

Michael pointed out again how fortunate I was for the life I lived caring for my children and getting to stay home with them... undeniably I was blessed. When he said goodbye and the door closed, my heart did more than break...it shattered. It had fallen for something it desperately longed for—but from someone forbidden to me.

I realized that hunting season that true love in a marriage is more important to me than I allowed myself to admit. I had gotten so good at pushing my feelings aside and keeping myself busy to the point that I had convinced myself that the desires of my heart were just fantasies that weren't meant to come true. That was until Michael put a twinkle in my eye, a smile on my face, and a spark back in my heart.

Why God brought such joy to my heart just to take it away, I didn't understand.

I locked myself in the bathroom to be alone and let my heart cry. Questions raced through my mind one after another…questions I didn't have answers to.

Why did God allow this man into my life when I was married and why did He allow my heart to have feelings for him? Other men paid me attention and complimented before. Why this time did I fall? Will Michael remain in my heart forever? Will I ever see him again? Why, if God is for marriages, did He seem so against mine? If God is all powerful and mighty, why then couldn't or wouldn't He give to me and Brad what I longed for in our marriage?

If God responded, I didn't hear.

I got angry and screamed on the inside, "What kind of God are You? Don't You care that I'm hurting?"

Still no answer….

"What's wrong with me?" I sobbed. "What makes my heart desire love the way it does and why am I so stubborn about wanting things my way?"

The silence frustrated me. I didn't want to get up off the floor; the motivation simply wasn't there. I wanted an understanding at that very moment as to what was going on in my life and an answer to where it was headed.

Silence lingered, but having heard no answer didn't give me permission to stay hidden from my children, clients, and the work that needed to be done. I was left with no choice but to pull myself to my feet and go about my day even if I didn't understand…even if an answer didn't come.

Perhaps your heart too is broken over something you deeply desire, but don't have. This can leave you feeling frustrated, stuck, and even hopeless. We mustn't stay down, though.

I gathered myself and came out of the bathroom. Jenna beamed with a smile of relief and ran to my arms when she saw me. The look on Eric's face was a look of concern. I didn't want my children to worry. I needed to be strong for them; they needed to know they could count on me.

> Strong people stand up for themselves. Stronger people stand up for others. (Chris Gardner)

The rest of the day wasn't easy to get through. I broke down several times thinking of and missing the joy that was brought to my heart that past week. I repeatedly reminded myself, however, of the blessings in my life to get back on track. I had two beautiful children to love and care for. I had parents that loved and supported me. My husband, our children, and I had our health, a home in the country, and more than we deserved. *How could I be so selfish and still want more?*

As my family and I traveled to church later that evening, a beckoning for true love wouldn't silence itself. I stared out the window praying silently for mercy while fighting back tears. For so long, I pleaded for love from Brad. Sadly, I found myself praying to be freed from my marriage and for a second chance, for I had fallen out of love. "Surely, God, You must care," my heart whispered, "please help me."

For a split second, I felt a spark of hope ignite in my heart that God would allow me a second chance at true love. I no more than embraced the thought of having the love I desired in a companion though and it was snatched by thoughts of being separated from my children if ever I left Brad. Fearing what I'd lose if I walked away from my promise, I prayed my heart would come to its senses and be true to my husband.

The following weeks grew to more of a struggle. Never before had I desired true love as much as I did then. My heart longed for a companion to go out of their way to show their love for me. It longed to be appreciated, to be held, and to be included. I woke desiring that kind of care and went to bed desiring it too. I wasn't okay. I hurt terribly and had grown weary of settling and "going without." I lost interest in hobbies I used to enjoy. I struggled to put one foot in front of the other to keep going. I felt stuck, trapped in a place I didn't want to be, and hopeless. My dream for the love I desired seemed out of reach. It wasn't worth losing my children. Plus, because of the promise I made, I believed it was my place to stay where I was even if God never intended for me to marry when I did.

I fell into a pit of self-pity and anger. I was angry at God for allowing me to follow through with marriage and angry at myself for getting married when my heart knew something wasn't right in the first place. I complained and felt sorry for myself day in and day out and then felt guilty and scolded myself for being picky and desiring more than I deserved. Had I not married, I wouldn't have my son and daughter that I love dearly. *What was it that made me believe there was more to life than what I had anyway? Why did I think I deserved more when so many were far worse off than me? Why couldn't I settle like my mom advised me and be thankful for what I had?* Had I not been so picky and such a dreamer, I wouldn't have been in the situation I was.

After lecturing myself, I pointed my finger back to God and accused Him of being heartless and mean. I was angry at Brad as well for not appreciating and loving me the way I needed as a wife and for the lack of attention and respect I felt he gave to our marriage. There seemed no end to this vicious cycle that went on and on. It left me feeling bitter and resentful. I found life to be exhausting.

"Where are You?" I cried out to God.

No matter how much I pleaded to God for answers and for my feelings for my husband to return, He remained silent and I continued drifting farther from Brad. I felt drained… I looked drained.

How much farther down could I get, I wondered, *and how was it that no one seemed to notice how much of a mess I was in?*

> *You know how troubled I am; You have kept a
> record of my tears. (Psalm 56:8 GNB)*

Then it happened. My parents must have sensed my spirit was broken. My mom reached out to me in my brokenness and encouraged me to me to pray. She offered devotionals to inspire me. I laid aside what she gave, complaining, "I've been praying… God doesn't care."

My attitude didn't stop my mom from reaching out to me and offering love and care. She and my dad must have been concerned to know I was struggling…how I wished they could ease the pain my broken heart was feeling with their hugs and the prayers they offered.

Soon after, a mission retreat was taking place at our church to which my mom invited me to go. I had no intention or interest in going, but I didn't have the heart to tell my mom, "No," and cause her to hurt.

Nothing during the retreat caught my attention. I was focused merely on getting back home to wallow in self-pity. Unexpectedly, though, a feeling came over me at the end of the service to stay and seek reconciliation. I had always found comfort in the sacrament of reconciliation, but even that no longer inspired me. The feeling, however, to stay was so strong I couldn't dismiss it with, "No, thanks."

I asked my mom if she'd watch over Eric and Jenna so I could go to confession.

I entered the confessional and sat face to face with the mission priest who traveled from another state to conduct the retreat. Not knowing where to begin, I broke into a sob. The priest asked why it had been so long since my last confession. His question caught me off guard, for he wouldn't have known how long it had been. Regardless, I confessed that I had given up on faith and lost desire in going to confession.

He asked why it was that I felt as though I did something wrong. Catching me off guard again, but not giving too much thought to how he knew, I confessed that I was married and had grown fond of another man. He shared that this man came into my life to bring me closer to God. He shared also that I felt unworthy and had been struggling in my marriage. He knew of the close relationship I had with my children and said God cautioned me not to get married, but I didn't listen.

Curious how this priest I'd never met before knew any of what he shared, I looked up with the intent to ask, "How do you know this?"

He responded, "God" before I had the chance to ask.

The priest went on to share that God would show me how much He loves me, that I would grow spiritually and teach others what God would teach me, and that I would live a fulfilled life.

I didn't know what to make of everything I was told. There was, however, a beautiful calmness that came over me as though the Lord's presence was near. The priest instructed me to read the tenth station of the cross for my penance and to pay attention to what God would tell me.

I was eager to go home and hear God speak. While on my way, I rehearsed the conversation over and over in my mind of what took place in the confessional and I wondered if others had an experience similar to mine.

As soon as I got home, I read the tenth station of the cross, "Jesus is stripped of His garments." I didn't understand. It went on to say we must strip ourselves of attachments we cling to that distance our relationship with God. I clung tightly to my children and my parents. *Was God asking me to let go of my parents and children?* I wondered. If so, that was more than I was willing to do. My children and parents meant the world to me. I feared losing my parents since I was little and I feared losing my children the moment they were born. Without the ones I loved the most, I didn't know how I would get along.

It seemed a voice from within whispered for me to read the tenth station from a different Stations of the Cross pamphlet I had lying on my dresser. Curious as to what message I'd discover, I read the tenth station from the booklet I was directed to. The writer described stripping ourselves of attachments such as hopelessness, self-pity, worry, fear, anxiety, control, and insecurity.

At that moment, an awakening took place in my soul…in my spirit.

From the time I could remember, I clung to insecurity, doubt, worry, fear, anxiety, and control, and now to unworthiness, self-pity, blame, and hopelessness without realizing the damage I was doing to my well-being and to my relationship with God. Not in all the years that I prayed and meditated on the Stations of the Cross had I ever understood the tenth station the way I did at that moment. God had my attention and responded after all this time!

> *I took my troubles to the LORD; I cried out to him, and he answered my prayer. (Psalm 120:1 NLT)*

I didn't want to continue going through life worrying, pitying myself, feeling sad and unworthy, and expecting the worst. I wanted to hear more of what God wanted to say. I felt led to see what was in the books my mom had given to me that I neglected to read. One of the devotionals shared this scripture:

> *Ask and it will be given to you; seek and you will find; knock and the door will be opened to you. For everyone who asks receives; the one who seeks finds; and to the one who knocks, the door will be opened. Which of you, if your son asks for bread, will give him a stone? Or if he asks for a fish, will give him a snake? If you then, though you are evil, know how to give good gifts to your children, how much more will your Father in heaven give good gifts to those who ask him! (Matthew 7:7–11 NIV)*

An excitement arose within me. *Could this be?* I wondered. *Could God really love me this much?* Other questions immediately arose. *What if my desire for true love in a companion is from God like*

I once believed? What if He wants to forgive me for the mistake I made and will give me a second chance after all?

I opened to scripture in the Bible prior to this one, but the words never made sense to me or spoke to my heart like the words had spoken to me that day. A peace came over me. My spirit came to life and ignited my soul with hope and confidence that indeed God loved me and would take care of me. Perhaps God was trying to tell me all the while that He loved me and would take care of me, but I was too stubborn to listen and too preoccupied with finding a solution on my own for my problem. Perhaps God was just waiting for me to reach the point that I was ready to listen. Perhaps He used others to get through to me, my mom being one of them. Whatever His plan, my eyes were opened and it felt good!

> *I have told you these things so that you will be*
> *filled with my joy. Yes, your joy will overflow! (John*
> *15:11 NLT)*

I realized it wasn't that my prayers fell deaf on God's ears like I believed all along, but rather the promptings of the Holy Spirit's that fell deaf on my ears and His presence that went unnoticed. Upon the realization and awakening in my spirit, regret also came over me. After all the good that God had done for me, prior to my brokenness in the pit, and the times He was faithful to come through for me, I still criticized His love and lacked faith instead of believing He'd continue to come through. I promised I wouldn't harden my heart toward God again or dismiss the help He sends from others who care about my well-being. I believed God cared and that I was worthy!

> *Understand this, my dear brothers and sisters:*
> *You must all be quick to listen, slow to speak, and*
> *slow to get angry. (James 1:19 NLT)*

POINTS TO PONDER

Are you relying on your own strength to fix a situation or on your own understanding to see a dream come to pass?

Perhaps you also are feeling stressed out and worried about a situation that God already has under control.

Do you feel unworthy of your heart's desires or blame God for a circumstance in your life?

Perhaps like me, you doubt God cares for you and you wonder if He will come through for you. Perhaps you as well have gone so far as to push Him away and fill a longing in your heart with something other than what God has to offer because you also cling to unnecessary attachments that make it difficult to tune in to the Holy Spirit's promptings.

My friend, God is not hiding from you and He is by all means, not mean or angry at you. He wants to be the One you turn to when you are hurting and afraid. He will back away, however, and let you attempt to find solutions to the struggles you are facing, if that's what you choose. No matter what mistakes you make, He will rescue you through His unfailing love and give you mercy and grace, for *Hebrews 4:16 (NLT)* says, *"So let us come boldly to the throne of our gracious God. There we will receive his mercy, and we will find grace to help us when we need it most."* Friend, our Lord has the answer to your circumstance, knows what is best for you, and wants what's best for you at all times. He's waiting for you to ask for your needs and to tell Him your fears; we have not because we ask not. It is not necessary that you know the solution to your situation. What matters is that you trust the Lord to guide you and that you follow where He leads.

> *Then when you call, the LORD will answer.*
> *'Yes, I am here,' he will quickly reply. (Isaiah 58:9 NLT)*

Prayer: Dear God, help me to reach out for help and to run to You, not from You, in times of struggle. Teach me to recognize Your voice. Forgive me please, for the times that I have failed to turn to

You as well as from others You have sent to help me. Forgive me also for the times that I have gotten angry and tried to do in my own strength what only You can do. Thank You for never giving up on me or turning Your back even when I fail and turn my back. Open my eyes to Your Word and help me to replace any unnecessary attachments or lies that I have been clinging to with the truth. Help me to rely on You and ask in prayer for my needs to be met. Help me to trust that You will come through for me and lead me where You want me to go. In Your name, Jesus, I pray. Amen.

Chapter 3

---⚜---

GOD CARES

*Jesus said to the people who believed in him, "You are truly
my disciples if you remain faithful to my teachings. And you
will know the truth, and the truth will set you free."*

—John 8:31–32 (NLT)

I wondered if other members from church experienced an unusual
confession during the retreat like I did. Whether yes or no, it didn't
matter. God had a purpose for me to experience what I did. He used
the mission priest to open my heart to truth and to give hope for my
future. My heart opened indeed; upon opening, it found hope to put
my trust in our Lord. Praise God, for when we know Jesus, we know
truth!

*I have told you these things so that you won't
abandon your faith. (John 16:1 NLT)*

A hunger for the truth and thirst for Jesus arose in my spirit.
I started teaching religious education to Eric. I learned God is all
good. He loves me more than I ever imagined and wants to bless me
in ways I never thought possible. I need only to make my requests
known to Him and trust in His love and care to provide for me.

I thought to myself how it must have hurt God when I told Him I wanted a real man to love me instead of Him. I believed He came to me in my dream to reveal that He wanted a personal relationship with me to fill what was missing in my life. I truly felt sorrow for the hurt I must have caused and regretted not having my heart opened to Jesus. I asked for forgiveness, invited the Lord into my circumstance, and committed to studying His Word. I prayed to let go of attachments that held me captive so I could have the life God intended.

The more I studied God's Word, the more hope I found in His promises. The more I hoped, the more I put my trust in our Lord to bless me with a life of abundance...a life I believed God wants for all. From this time on, the past fifteen-plus years of feeling "less than," insignificant, and unworthy began to unravel as my journey of letting go of one lie at a time and replacing them with truth began.

After several months of having opened my heart and believing God's promises were meant for me, the awakening in my spirit was obvious. Brad saw confidence he'd never seen in me before... confidence that made me shine and walk with my head held higher. I wondered if my confidence may have felt as a threat to him; I was compared to my sister, Mary, who was known for standing her ground no matter the circumstance. By the tone of Brad's voice, the resemblance between Mary and me seemed to be displeasing to him. Because I sensed judgement and condemnation, doubt arose in my spirit. I went from believing I'd have a second chance at love to fearing I'd remain unsatisfied in marriage.

What was I thinking? I thought. What my heart longed for was impossible. Surely, there'd be times I'd have to be apart from my children to share them with their father if ever I left Brad. I couldn't bear the thought of not being with Eric and Jenna like I was used to. They needed me, I believed, and I needed them. How I'd provide financially was another concern. Hopelessness replaced my trust that God could make the impossible possible. Unworthiness replaced my hope of believing God would grant me His mercy.

There I sat feeling trapped and full of self-pity. Perhaps because I reconnected with attachments that God commanded for me to release. My heart was heavy and tired from carrying the load of "what ifs" and worries I wasn't meant to carry.

I curled up in the bathtub of water listening to a CD Mary had just given to me. Feeling doomed because it truly appeared there was no way out of the circumstance I had gotten myself into, I bowed my head and prayed for acceptance of the decision I made on my wedding day. Suddenly, the song, "He Will Make a Way," by Don Moen started playing. The lyrics caught my attention as the artist sang about God being able to make a way where there seems to be no way even though it seems hopeless.

A spark of hope flickered once again in my spirit. It was as though God was speaking right to my heart during that song…as though He played it just for me for that very moment to keep believing that with God, all things are possible no matter how impossible my request seemed.

But how…how could God make a way with my situation when there truly seemed to be no way? My concerns seemed too big…too much to ask. Brad would have rights to our children. I would need a job suitable for my circumstances as a single mom to provide for Eric and Jenna. Between having to share them with their dad and more than likely having to be out of the home for a job to provide, there'd be little time to spend with the ones dearest to me. *And where would we live? What would I drive? Who would help if my house or my car needed repair?* It simply seemed too much to ask and hope.

> *For I am the LORD your God who takes hold*
> *of your right hand and says to you, Do not fear; I*
> *will help you. (Isaiah 41:13 NIV)*

While questions went through my mind, it was easy to be convinced there was no way God could make possible my requests. *What if though…what if God indeed used that song to speak to my heart and give confirmation that I had reason to hope and to believe He would do the impossible?*

Perhaps you too are struggling with a situation where there seems to be no way. Or perhaps you're allowing your concerns to outweigh the goodness and power of our Lord.

I thought back to the worry and concern of previous circumstances in my life such as the safety of my unborn baby during my first pregnancy, finding a suitable job while wanting to be a stay-at-home mom, how I'd manage to get through the hunting season, staying well during my second pregnancy, and the anxiety I experienced from my son going off to kindergarten. God had come through for all these circumstances and provided above and beyond.

My thoughts then drifted to prayers and requests that went unanswered for my husband and me. Ever since Brad's marriage proposal, I had been praying for him to love me the way I hoped to be loved, but to no avail, my prayers and requests went unanswered. I pondered on thoughts as to why my marriage continued to be a struggle. As a wife, I didn't know what more I could have done to please Brad other than what I had been doing for the past ten-plus years. I wondered if perhaps God had other plans for me than the life I hoped I'd have with Brad.

While reflecting on prayers that were answered and prayers that weren't, I thought back also to a time when doubt crept into my spirit and fear kept me from a dream I had my heart set on. It was my senior year in high school when I began making plans for the career I felt called to do. From the time I could remember, I wanted to be a counselor to encourage people to believe in their dreams. I wanted to build confidence in people to face their challenges. I felt this knowing in my spirit that I was meant to make a positive impact on the lives of many.

While planning for college and my dream career, however, three small words, "You…a counselor?" popped into my mind and caught my attention. The taunting tone of those three little words left me to doubt my self-worth and second guess what I believed was my calling. I then recalled events as a young girl that I looked forward to that had ended in disappointment. I thought perhaps my hope to be a counselor would end in disappointment as well.

Because I focused back then on letdowns from the past, I allowed the seeds of doubt and unworthiness to take root in my spirit and replace my dream with fear. Without realizing it, I put restrictions on God, neglected my dream, and let it fall by the wayside. I settled for an education in Fashion and Retail Management at a small college, which left me with a sense of dishonor toward my heart.

> *The god of this age has blinded the minds of unbelievers, so that they cannot see the light of the gospel that displays the glory of Christ, who is the image of God. (2 Corinthians 4:4 NIV)*

Upon acknowledging my regret for not staying true to my heart's desire to be counselor, I recalled my confession with the mission priest and pondered on the tenth station of the cross. I let go of my dream back then because I clung to attachments that held me back. For too long, I carried a load I wasn't meant to carry.

I wasn't about to let unnecessary attachments continue to steal the desires of my heart. Somehow, someway, I needed to strip myself of doubt, worry, and fear if I wanted to see my dreams come to pass and trust wholeheartedly that God would make a way where there seemed to be no way.

I clung to the belief that God used the song, "He Will Make A Way," to encourage me and to build my trust and faith in Him. I played it over and over, letting the words soak into my spirit. I meditated on God's promise in *Ephesians 3:20 (NKJV)*, *"Now to Him who is able to do exceedingly abundantly above all that we ask or think, according to the power that works in us."*

I thanked my sister for the song she shared with me and expressed what an impact it made on my spirit. I shared that I felt neglected and broken from feeling as though my needs as a wife went unnoticed. I shared also that I reached the end of the rope and wanted out of my marriage. I admitted that I was terrified of the unknown and of what the outcome of my circumstance would be if I left Brad. Mary took me under her wings and promised to walk with me so I wouldn't fall. I turned to another sister, Loretta, who offered support through listening and praying and to my sister, Kate, who encouraged me to listen to the promises God placed in my heart. My sisters helped me to keep focused on the power of God instead of the concerns of my situation.

I shared my struggle with my parents as well. I confessed my fear to them and asked for prayer to stand strong in my faith. They expressed their concern as they knew my spirit had been broken. My dad handwrote the *Jabez Prayer* from the Bible and encouraged me to pray it every day: *"And Jabez called on the God of Israel saying, 'Oh, that You would bless me indeed, and enlarge my territory, that Your hand would be with me, and that You would keep me from evil, that I may not cause pain!' So God granted him what he requested"* (1 Chronicles 4:10 NKJV).

My dad's gesture was small, but his care and concern for my faith and well-being sincerely touched my heart. The scripture, *"Ask and it will be given to you; seek and you will find; knock and the door will be opened to you. For everyone who asks receives; the one who seeks finds; and to the one who knocks, the door will be opened. Which of you, if your son asks for bread, will give him a stone? Or if he asks for a fish, will give him a snake? If you then, though you are evil, know how to give good gifts to your children, how much more will your Father in heaven give good gifts to those who ask him!"* (Matthew 7:7–11 NIV) that awakened my spirit for the first time a while back appeared again in my devotionals on that same day my dad gave me the *Jabez Prayer*. I believed God was inviting me to turn to Him and to trust that He will provide.

I was grateful for the love and mercy God offered me through the support from my family; I needed every bit of it as fear was a strong and mighty weapon the devil continuously used against me. *John 16:33 (NLT)*, however, says this: *"Here on earth you will have many trials and sorrows. But take heart, because I have overcome the world."*

I vowed to hold tight to God's promises and push through all that was holding me back. I prayed the *Jabez Prayer* fervently that God would bless my children and me indeed and spare us from more than we could bear.

Within weeks of receiving the *Jabez Prayer*, my mom gave me a Christmas ornament. It was a little, white box with a red ribbon on it. She said the ornament caught her eye so she bought one for each of my siblings and me. I hung the ornament on my Christmas tree and happened to come across an encouraging story, *The Parable of the Blessing Box,* by Steve Watkins, only days after receiving the present from my mom. The story was about a man who died and went to heaven. When the man reached heaven, he noticed a white box with his name on it. Inside of the box were blessings God wanted to give the man, but because the man never asked for them, he never received them.

The Parable of the Blessing Box inspired me to believe our Lord wants to grant us the desires of our hearts. I had grown weary of telling myself lies that I was okay and that my heart needs to settle. The inspiring story brought special meaning to the ornament from my mom and ignited my spirit to believe there was more to life than what I had been living. I was inspired also to believe that if indeed what we ask for is in line with God's Word, our Lord will pour forth His blessings upon us. Not wanting to miss out on what God had in store for me, it was my intent to run to His arms and ask boldly for the desires of my heart.

> *Therefore I tell you, whatever you ask for in prayer, believe that you have received it, and it will be yours. (Mark 11:24 NIV)*

Since I was aware that not all desires of the heart come from God, I prayed for discernment. My friend, a pastor, puts it this way, "Part of wisdom is discerning which desires are from God and which are not. To do this, we are to compare every thought and desire with God's Word." He explains that praying in faith includes praying, "Thy will be done," and trusting that whatever answer and blessing given is truly best for us, even if it is not the answer or blessing we wanted. He goes on to say that when God does not give us what we ask for, it's because He intends to give us something better. "It's like writing to Mom," he says, "and asking for ten dollars, and she writes back, 'No, but here's twenty dollars instead.'"

Because I didn't want to desire anything out of God's will. I asked in His name, for the desires of my heart to be aligned with His will. I turned to scripture to help align my thoughts with truth. I prayed for hope to remain when fear attacked.

Through scripture, taking notes, and journaling, I came to know our Lord and began to develop a relationship with Him rather than just know of Him. It became apparent to me that God will allow certain struggles in our lives, some of which will be consequences due to mistakes we make, to draw us closer to Him and grow us stronger through His love. As I grew in our Lord's love, I gained strength and found hope through spending time with Him. Because of the struggle I was going through, I developed a deeper relationship with our Lord and a stronger passion to encourage others who may be going through a difficult time. After all, who better to teach someone than one who actually went through the experience?

> *Praise be to the God and Father of our Lord Jesus Christ, the Father of compassion and the God of all comfort, who comforts us in all our troubles, so that we can comfort those in any trouble with the comfort we ourselves receive from God. (2 Corinthians 1:3–4 NIV)*

While dealing with my circumstance, I worked toward embracing the lessons I was given, looking for the good that came from my circumstance and being appreciative of the little things while being careful not to take what I had for granted. I kept my eyes open for others who may be in need of encouragement, for *1 Thessalonians 5:11 (ESV)* says, *"Therefore encourage one another and build one another up, just as you are doing."*

In my attempt to do what I felt inspired to do, I found a friend in someone I hadn't expected. He was Brad's friend who was going through a difficult time as well. I reached out to comfort, console, and encourage my new friend, Larry. In doing so, I found myself focusing less and less on my situation and more on teaching the goodness and sovereignty of our Lord. I believed there truly was purpose for my struggle which brought a spirit of courage and joy to my heart.

And we know that in all things God works for the good of those who love him, who have been called according to his purpose. (Romans 8:28 NIV)

That Christmas I wrote a letter to God, asking for the desires of my heart to be granted, for *1 John 5:14 (ESV)* says, *"And this is the confidence that we have toward him, that if we ask anything according to his will he hears us."* I confessed my failures, expressed my need for our Lord, and asked Him to lead me to the life He had in store. I asked for strength to embrace my struggle and do what I needed to do.

Embracing my circumstances wasn't always easy.

The time came that Brad learned I had grown fond of Michael, the hunter who stayed at our house. A letter that I had written to Michael was discovered. That was a difficult day. I felt ashamed of my sin, much like the woman who was caught in adultery in *John 8:1–11* may have felt when the teachers of the law and the Pharisees made her stand before the group and Jesus to be judged. I hurt for my husband, for I confessed to him how unhappy I had been and that I couldn't pretend any longer to be okay. I shared that as a wife I wanted to be more than a homemaker; that my heart had been lonely for too long, and that my love for him had grown cold. It saddened me to see what I saw in Brad's eyes, a hurt I'd never seen before. For so long I waited for his love…now that he realized what he had lost, he was the one hurting.

Brad appeared angry and indicated that I had no grounds for divorce, if that's what I wanted. He pointed out that we are not pardoned from the commitment of marriage just because of how we feel. It is so that we are not excused from the promise of marriage just because we no longer "feel" the love we once felt in our hearts, for *Mark 10:9 (NIV)* clearly states, *"Therefore what God has joined together, let no one separate."*

Knowing this, and reflecting on *Ephesians 5:24 (NIV)* that says, *"Now as the church submits to Christ, so also wives should submit to their husbands in everything,"* was reason for me to feel condemned and to believe it was my place to stay where I was despite my heartache. However, *Ephesians 5:25 (NIV)* goes on to say, *"Husbands, love your wives, just as Christ loved the church and gave himself up for her."*

There wasn't anything I wouldn't have done for Brad or for another. I thrived on giving of my time, doing for others, and submitting out of love. It simply warmed my heart to see others happy. I questioned though the example I was giving to my children by staying married and continuing to submit to their father, for my spirit had weakened from feeling neglected throughout the years. Not only had I questioned the quality of life for my children, but for all of us. I wanted what was best for my family…at the time though, I wasn't sure what that was.

I learned through experience that every action has a consequence, either good or bad, depending on the action. Surely, I didn't want to continue making poor choices that would lead to continued suffering and an unfulfilled life.

I turned to my priest for counsel and began by confessing my sin as a wife. Forgiveness was my first step. *Ephesians 4:31–32 (NIV)* says, *"Get rid of all bitterness, rage and anger, brawling and slander, along with every form of malice. Be kind and compassionate to one another, forgiving each other, just as in Christ God forgave you."*

It wasn't just Brad I needed to forgive. I needed to forgive my father-in-law, who had passed away. My dad cautioned me about forgiving after I shared a dream that I had about my father-in-law coming back to life.

"Never!" I said to my dad after he advised me to forgive my father-in-law.

My dad explained, however, that we are forgiven as much as we forgive and in order for me to be forgiven, I needed to forgive whoever wronged me. *Matthew 6:14 (NLT)* states: *"If you forgive those who sin against you, your heavenly Father will forgive you."* The priest encouraged forgiveness toward my father-in-law as well. "When we don't forgive," he cautioned, "we fall short of grace."

> *See to it that no one falls short of the grace of God and that no bitter root grows up to cause trouble and defile many. (Hebrew 12:15 NIV)*

I knew I was supposed to forgive; it just wasn't in my heart to forgive my father-in-law. We didn't see eye-to-eye. I was angry and bitter toward him. I blamed him for the way I felt treated by his son. The priest, however, prayed with me and offered a forgiveness prayer to pray every day. The prayer was quite lengthy and covered everything from forgiving our parents, siblings, and teachers from an early age on up to forgiving those who recently caused us pain.

I prayed the prayer to forgive and can honestly say the anger, revenge, and resentment I had toward Brad and my father-in-law lifted from my spirit within a matter of weeks. I was able to acknowledge wounds from my past and forgive with an understanding that neither Brad nor my father-in-law's intention was ever to cause hurt. I also acknowledged the unnecessary blame I had been putting on Brad and even God for my unhappiness for so long. A new love for my husband formed in my heart…not a love between a husband and a wife, but a love like that between a brother and a sister in Christ.

> *Strive for peace with everyone, and for the holiness without which no one will see the Lord. (Hebrews 12:14 ESV)*

In the weeks that followed, I took more seriously what I was teaching my children by staying married to their dad. It became obvious that Brad and I had simply been going through the actions of a married couple and set a pattern in motion…a pattern I didn't want carried over into my children's future. Clearly, both my husband and I lacked the maturity and responsibility needed prior to our marriage commitment which allowed dysfunction in our lives, the lives of our children, and in our home. I didn't want either of my children to settle one day for a marriage that their father and I had.

As I gave thought to the life I had been living and the future for my children, I meditated on *John 10:10 (NKJV), "The thief does not come except to steal, and to kill, and to destroy. I have come that they may have life, and that they may have it more abundantly."*

A desire burned within for freedom of the unsatisfying life I had been living. Not knowing the outcome of my circumstance or what freedom would cost me was terrifying however, as was the thought of being on my own to provide for my children. I didn't see a way that I'd ever have courage to stand on my own.

Not only was I frightened of what may lie ahead, I didn't want Brad to hurt, for I had never been the kind to turn and walk away from someone who hurt. I needed the direction of God in my life more than ever. I needed to know what to do for the sake of my children, my husband, and for myself. I knew better this time that the answer to my situation was not to plan for another baby like I did prior to fill a void in my heart. I had grown wiser. I grew to be a better listener as well, so I did what I knew to do… I prayed and listened for God to show me the way and to help Brad and me through this difficult time.

Show me the right path, O LORD; point out
the road for me to follow. (Psalm 25:4 NLT)

I dreamed dreams. I dreamed of being trapped in a large building with white walls and what appeared to be military men dressed in white. I wanted out and searched desperately in the dark for freedom while the men were sleeping. At last I found a door, but was spotted by what seemed to be a guard. The man told me I wasn't free to go. Refusing to give up, I searched again the following evening for a way out of the building while the men were asleep. Again, the guard stopped me and said I wasn't free to go. By the third attempt the next evening to seek freedom, I hung my head and said, "I know…this is my place," when the man approached me. This time, however, I heard, "Let her go. She's been wanting out for eight years." I wasted no time in running for the large garage-like door. A radiant light beamed on the other side as it opened. Once freed, I stood with my arms open wide in awe of the beauty of a green pasture with flowers and a stream. Surprised that I was alone, I said, "I didn't want to be alone." A man's voice from behind then spoke, "I know" as he placed his hand on my shoulder. This man, who appeared to be Jesus, took my hand, and together we walked down a path.

The following night, I dreamed I was running on a mountain looking for a place to hide from a man who was chasing me. I hid inside the nearest crevice large enough for me to fit and trembled with sheer terror, for I knew the man was quickly approaching and I'd have to face him. Instead of having to face him, however, the mountain surprisingly erupted and I was safe in the arms of another man who appeared again to me as our Savior.

A third dream appeared in my sleep. Again, I was running in terror from a man who was chasing me, this time near a gas station. I ran so fast to keep from being caught, took a turn around a corner, and simultaneously, ran right into the arms of the same Christ-like being as the gas station blew up in flames.

What it was that I was running from, I wasn't exactly sure. *Was it an actual being or was it the fear from the storm I was facing?* Perhaps it was a storm still on the way that I was running from… I wasn't given an answer.

Whatever it was, I was inspired and given hope through my dreams. Through them, I believed God revealed Himself by assuring me that He was by my side and would help me get where I was meant to be. I sensed in my spirit that God was preparing me for the challenges in my marriage to increase, but that there was nothing to fear. It all seemed so easy in my dreams… *If only it would be that easy in real life*, I thought.

I shared what happened in my dreams with the priest to pursue an understanding of what God was telling me through them. He didn't know for certain. I went home and prayerfully turned to God and asked Him earnestly if the thoughts I had of being free from my marriage were thoughts from Him or thoughts from the devil. I then opened my Bible to the page where I left off the previous day from my Bible study. I was taken to *Matthew 14:22–36*, the story of Jesus walking on the water when Peter and the disciples were on the boat during the fourth watch of the night. *"But immediately Jesus spoke to them, saying, 'Be of good cheer! It is I; do not be afraid'" (Matthew 14:27 NKJV).*

Peace settled in my heart. I sensed even stronger in my spirit that indeed a challenge was up ahead, but that God was with me and would rescue me during the storm just as He did in my dreams. I was well aware that often times a test comes with challenges that we face and that it will require us to hold tight to our Lord's promises and to our faith. No one enjoys having to go through the test, me included. But I was learning through reading scripture and devotionals and even my experiences that God goes with us in these challenges that we come out a better, stronger person because of the challenge and that a little faith goes a long way.

> *And the God of all grace, who called you to*
> *his eternal glory in Christ, after you have suffered a*
> *little while, will himself restore you and make you*
> *strong, firm and steadfast. (1 Peter 5:10 NIV)*

I was under the understanding that there wasn't going to be a way around, under, or over my circumstance. But rather, if I was going to pass my test of faith and be what God created me to be, I was going to have to face my fears while leaning on God and walk through the storm.

> *Truly I tell you, if you have faith as small as a*
> *mustard seed, you can say to this mountain, "Move*
> *from here to there, and it will move. Nothing will*
> *be impossible for you." (Matthew 17:20 NIV)*

POINTS TO PONDER

Is there someone in your life who you've been struggling to forgive?

Is there a lie you believe or attachments you cling to that are holding you back from the desires in your heart? If so, what would it take to live the dream you desire to live and how would that change your life?

Perhaps you're struggling with a situation that seems hopeless or impossible to overcome and you carry the unnecessary weight of the burden you've allowed it to become. It may even feel as though God has forgotten you. He hasn't. *Isaiah 49:16 (NASB)* says, *"Behold, I have inscribed you on the palms of My hands; Your walls are ever before Me."* Nothing is impossible for God. It is promised in *Matthew 19:26 (NIV)*: *"Jesus looked at them and said, 'With man this is impossible, but with God all things are possible.'"*

My friend, the enemy will try to convince you that you'll never make it, you're undeserving, it's your fault, and you need not forgive. Come to Jesus instead. Give to Him all your burdens and any unforgiveness in your heart. Trust with your entire being that our Lord does indeed care for you and that He can make possible what looks to be impossible. Remember, it's not up to you to find the solution to your struggle. Let God be God and show you the way. He wants to bless you and use you to help others.

> *Have I not commanded you? Be strong and courageous. Do not be afraid, do not be discouraged, for the LORD your God will be with you wherever you go. (Joshua 1:9 NIV)*

Prayer: Heavenly Father, thank You that You care for me and that nothing is impossible or too hard for You. Thank You for Your guidance through Your promises, a song, or an encouraging word through a friend or loved one. Help me to recognize any unnecessary baggage that I may be carrying. Forgive me for the times I have taken my focus off You and placed it on the storm I may be facing. Forgive me for the times I've not taken responsibility of my actions, but instead placed blame on others. Align my heart with Your will, give me the courage to turn from the enemy and to come boldly to You at all times asking for the desires of my heart. Help me to replace any hopelessness that I may feel with trust in Your promises and any unworthiness with a knowing that I am worthy. Help me to stay focused on Your love and power rather than the storm I may be facing. Help me to forgive so that I too may be forgiven and help me to let You be You and to continue to show me the way. In the name of Jesus, I pray. Amen.

Chapter 4

WATCH

He gives power to the weak and strength to the powerless.

—Isaiah 40:29 (NLT)

While I continued to pray for discernment and God's direction for my life, my desire for Brad's attention lessened more and more. Brad, on the other hand, appeared insecure and desperate for the "me" I used to be. I didn't want to remain that insecure, self-conscious, "please everyone" kind of person that I had been. Now that my spirit awakened to truth and hope, my intentions were to honor the work that God had done in my heart and the change it brought to my spirit.

This change in me led to lengthy and unpleasant conversations late into the night as Brad attempted to win me back. My heart was set on the direction I believed God was leading, but since my heart was sensitive to other's pain, it was difficult for me to take a stand to my husband and hold my ground.

I couldn't honor what God was doing, however, and please Brad at the same time, for God does not want us to please to the point of compromising His will for us. *Galatians 1:10 (NIV)* says, *"Am I now trying to win the approval of human beings, or of God? Or am I trying to please people? If I were still trying to please people, I would not be a servant of Christ."*

I offered my weaknesses to the Lord and prayed for strength for both Brad and me to endure what was to come. I tried to hide the tension between us from Eric and Jenna by turning to my parents and sisters for support during moments of despair. I continued praying, desiring more and more time with the Lord; spending time with Him lifted my spirits and brought hope and peace into a situation that once appeared hopeless.

As the deer longs for streams of water, so I long
for you, O God. (Psalm 42:1 NLT)

Jenna, at the age of two, was busy nonstop, appearing to be her "happy-go-lucky" self. Eric, on the other hand, seemed to struggle. After arriving to school ill a couple of days in a row, I took him to our doctor and was scheduled an appointment with a counselor who she recommended. My heart was heavy for what I was sure Eric was experiencing.

As I suspected, Eric shared with the counselor that he was concerned. He expressed that he worried during his bus ride to school about what was taking place between his mom and dad. It broke my heart to know Eric was concerned and obviously hurting. I knew, from experience, how worry can torment oneself. I didn't want either of my children living worried. I imagined how I would have been concerned about my mom or dad had either of them struggled. I needed to care for myself so I could take care of my children properly.

I reassured Eric that everything would be all right, that he and his sister would be taken care of, and that the counselor was there to help. Eric appeared to be more at peace after visiting with the counselor and being assured. He shared that he learned secrets give tummy aches. They sure do. I encouraged him and his sister to please share if ever something is bothering them. I promised there's nothing that will make me turn my back on them just as God will never turn His back on us.

At this point, I lost the spirit to submit myself to my marriage. It was my goal to continue my relationship with the Lord and care for the well-being of my children. Wanting to make certain that my heart was in line with God's will, I asked Him for a sign of confirmation.

Therefore the Lord himself will give you a sign.
(Isaiah 7:14 ESV)

While preparing dinner only days later, it seemed that within me I was cautioned, "Prepare for battle." I stopped what I was doing and looked around the room as though I'd be given a sign of what battle. After a moment of silence, I went back to fixing dinner. "Remain strong. Don't accept guilt," arose in my inner being. I didn't understand, but nor did I feel concerned.

Later that evening, Brad brought it to my attention that I was going against God's will if I was considering divorce. I disliked those late-night conversations. They were long and left me to feel guilty. That night, however, I recalled the words from earlier in the day to remain strong and not accept guilt. I remained then, firm in my belief that I was on the right track.

Be on your guard; stand firm in the faith; be
courageous; be strong. (1 Corinthians 16:13 NIV)

Though thankful for the sign of confirmation, the heated discussion left a draining effect on me in which I needed my thoughts realigned with truth as well as encouragement to keep hope. I resorted to my hideaway, the bathroom, to be alone with God. While there, I rocked myself back and forth on the floor and prayed again for another sign to be given if my children and I would be provided for and if one day, I'd have the love from a companion that my heart longed for.

I woke in the morning with a fine, silvery dust I noticed on my hand. Without giving the shimmering sparkles much attention, I quickly washed my hands and face and drove to town for Eric's baseball practice. After arriving home, I went to wash my hands to prepare lunch and noticed I still had sparkles on my hand. I looked in the mirror and saw I had sparkles around my eyes as well. "What is this?" I asked, without actually expecting an answer, but clearly heard within my spirit the words, "Angel dust."

I hadn't heard of angel dust before. Curious, of course, I gathered sparkles from around my eyes with clear packaging tape and headed back to town with my children to share with our priest and to inquire about the sparkling dust.

The priest seemed intrigued when I asked him what the sparkles were. He shared that it looked like angel dust and that he has only seen it on a rare occasion at a funeral. He questioned what happened the evening before. I explained that I asked God for a sign if it was so that He would provide for my children and me as well as bless me with the love I longed for. The priest asked why I thought the angel dust appeared on my left hand. My thought was because the marriage band goes on the left hand. He said he believed so too and then asked why I thought the angel dust appeared around my eyes. I thought back to the awakening I experienced after my confession with the mission priest and said, "Because my eyes have been opened to truth." He agreed with my belief and shared that God doesn't give us any greater sign than that of angel dust that He and His angels are working for us.

For he will order his angels to protect you wherever you go. (Psalm 91:11 NLT)

My visit with the priest gave me hope—hope that my prayers would be answered. I trusted God's promise in *Matthew 6:26–27 (NIV)* that He would provide, *"Look at the birds of the air; they do not sow or reap or store away in barns, and yet your heavenly Father feeds them. Are you not much more valuable than they?"*

My walk with the Lord had grown from discovering truth one day about God into believing that what mattered to me, mattered to Him, and likewise, what mattered to God, mattered to me. I would sit on the kitchen floor when the sun shone through the window and close my eyes to soak in the peace and calm I felt in that present moment. It was as though God's radiant love and power shone through me. I longed for moments with God. I praised Him for the good He gave and for the good that was on the way. I enjoyed heart-to-heart conversations with Him throughout my day and truly believed He was walking next to me just as it appeared in my dreams. My strength and hope came from the Lord.

By now it was the summer; Eric turned eight years old and Jenna three. I found joy in our usual summer activities together, riding the four-wheeler, playing outside, and making memories with my parents on their farm and at the cabin, fishing with them. I found joy also in the innocence of my children. For Mother's Day that year, Eric asked if I'd like a "#7 mom" necklace because the previous year he gave me a necklace that said "#1 mom" on it… I think he caught on that #1 is the best when I told him I want to stay a #1 mom in his heart forever.

That summer, I drove Eric and Jenna to swimming lessons in a nearby town. Their treat after swimming was to stop by the drive-in for lunch and an ice cream cone. One day while waiting for our lunch, a man approached us and asked where the window was to place an order. I thought it odd that he asked because the window was in clear view of where he was standing at the time of his request. The man and I shared conversation until our order arrived.

While visiting, the stranger made a comment that he sensed something holding me back from my calling. Curious as to why he said that, I asked if he was from the area. His response, "No…just passing through," made me believe that our encounter was divinely ordered. The stranger left me with a piece of advice, "Watch, listen, and learn." With that, our order was ready, so my children and I got in the truck to head back home. Both Eric and I looked mysteriously at each other and said, "It's like he was an angel."

> An unexpected situation could well lead to
> a divine appointment; any divine appointment
> will bring divine blessing! (Palitha Jayasooriya)

After clinging to "my way" the twelve years I had been married and trying to fix what was out of my control, I came to the realization that I may not live the life God intended if I stayed in a marriage that I questioned if I should have committed to. I recalled advice given from Michael, who I had fallen for. He encouraged me to honor my heart. At the time he shared, I didn't understand, but understood later that honoring one's heart is to respect and hold value to that still, small voice within our spirit where God speaks to us; otherwise known as our conscience, the compass to our soul.

> *A person's spirit is the lamp of the LORD; it searches throughout one's innermost being. (Proverbs 20:27 ISV)*

I was convinced that I dishonored my heart when I ignored that still, small voice when God tried to warn me about marrying. I prayed that I would pay closer attention, be a better listener, and have courage to honor the voice of God when He spoke to my heart.

> *Trust in the Lord with all your heart, and lean not on your own understanding; in all your ways acknowledge Him, and He shall direct your paths. (Proverbs 3:5–6 NKJV)*

I didn't know how to explain to my children that I had been considering leaving their dad. I didn't want to worry or disappoint either of them. I wondered, too, how I would tell Brad that I believed I dishonored my heart by getting married. He already seemed on the verge of breaking. I was concerned of what would happen if I left him.

I did what I knew to do. I prayed for a sign of confirmation if indeed I was being prepared to walk away from a promise I made despite the warnings I was given. I also prayed for the support of my children and for acceptance from my husband.

Fear stepped in and told me that I'd never make it on my own, that my children would blame me, I'd never be loved, wasn't pretty enough, and that I simply wasn't worthy. A feeling within my spirit, however, told me I would soar, I was loved, and that I had a purpose. Instead of giving into fear and listening to the negative voices, I waited patiently for God's response while holding tightly to what hope and faith I had.

> *For God hath not given us the spirit of fear;*
> *but of power, and of love, and of a sound mind. (2*
> *Timothy 1:7 KJV)*

While I waited, I pictured my parents and children seeing me laugh, seeing me loved and in love, seeing me whole, healthy and vibrant, and watching me soar above what tried to hold me down. I pictured myself living in a clean and simple home with a tidy yard. I saw myself encouraging and inspiring others as I had always dreamed!

During my wait, I continued to enjoy spending time with my parents and treasured opportunities with my children. Eric was in second grade, enjoyed school, and liked it when I brought treats to his class and did class projects with them. Jenna and Jamie, age three, were of age to start preschool, so I got back to volunteering for Head Start. Between visiting Eric's classroom and being involved with Head Start, I was on the go. I enjoyed watching Jenna interact with other children at preschool just as I did when Eric was in the program.

Our fifth hunting season was on its way. I lacked motivation that season to cook and clean for the hunters. But I pushed my way through it…it was my place for the time being.

Christmas came along and my spirits lifted. I enjoyed baking Christmas cookies with my children, watching Eric perform at school and in church for his programs, shopping for presents, and wrapping them. I enjoyed playing in the snow with my children, watching our favorite Christmas shows, and celebrating the Christmas Mass and traditions with my family.

The rest of the school year passed quickly. Before I knew it, I was running to Eric's baseball games again, taking my children to swimming lessons, and taking in outdoor activities.

When school started back up in the fall, Eric entered the third grade and was nine years old. Jenna was four years old, back in pre-school, and growing more and more social with friends at school. She was a leader at her young age. I so appreciated volunteering at Head Start and having the opportunity to watch Jenna learn and grow there and still make friends of my own. It was a positive experience for both of us.

Another hunting season came along-the sixth already. My heart felt even less of a desire that year than the previous one to operate the business, and still less of a desire to remain married. I made it through that season too, but was growing weary from the circumstance with my marriage and still no sign of confirmation from God that I was supposed to move in the direction I believed I was headed. It seemed the journey I was on was getting to be too much for too long. Yet there remained a flicker of hope within me, a "knowing" so to speak, in my soul, that God would come through for me.

I cried out, "I'm tired, Lord," in hopes for my burden to be lifted, for *Matthew 11:28–30 (NIV)* declares, *"Come to me, all you who are weary and burdened, and I will give you rest. Take my yoke upon you and learn from me, for I am gentle and humble in heart, and you will find rest for your souls. For my yoke is easy and my burden is light."*

Brad asked at this time for us to seek counsel with our priest. I agreed to do so. The priest knew the journey had been long already. I continued to pray the prayer that my dad hand wrote for me, continued studying God's Word, journaled, and listened to Christian music to feed my spirit and keep my hope alive.

Some days I was filled with hope for what was to come; other days I struggled to trust and stay in peace. There were days too that I felt selfish for not being satisfied with what I had and still wanting more. God had blessed me with so much already with the children I was given and the family I grew up with… It seemed greedy to want more. Yet God's Word says in *John 10:10 (ESV)* that Jesus came to give us life and to live it abundantly with more than we could ever ask. *"The thief comes only to steal and kill and destroy. I came that they may have life and have it abundantly."*

Because I truly believed God's Word that Jesus came to give a life of abundance, I continued to pray for direction, thanked Jesus for His love, goodness, and blessings, and clung to hope to live a life fulfilled.

In early January, Eric came to me with a piece of paper. He said, "I made this for your birthday, but something told me to give it to you now."

Eric's gift was a picture of a rainbow in the sky that he colored with a poem he had written called, *Don't Look Back*. It read: "*When things get hard and troubled, relationships don't turn out right. Run, but don't look back. I know it is hard, but God will help you as you go through it. You need to trust God what He says.*"

I was moved…more than words could say. My birthday was still three months away. Unable to hold back my tears, I took my son into my arms and thanked him from the bottom of my heart for his precious gift. "Where did you find the words to your poem?" I asked.

"I don't know," he said, "they just came to me."

I couldn't believe what just happened. I believed that God used my son for the encouragement, support, and direction I was looking for. God knew I was growing weary and waiting for a sign of confirmation as to whether to stay committed to my marriage. I believed He had a plan to assure me that He'd make a way where there didn't seem to be a way before I even had the problem. God is good!

I shared with Eric that his dad and I had been struggling. Eric appeared to understand. I knew his sister was too young for what I was convinced needed to be done; however, I believed it was time to start preparing for a change that I believed would be taking place.

Eric had two requests. Number one, that he and his sister go with me, and number two, that I be nice to his dad. I promised to honor his requests.

I loved my son's heart. It was gentle, mindful of others, and filled with love…he was wise for his young age.

But the wisdom that comes from heaven is first
of all pure; then peace-loving, considerate, submis-

sive, full of mercy and good fruit, impartial and sin-cere. (James 3:17 NIV)

I was reminded of *Matthew 6:26–27* that God cares about everything, even the birds, so surely He cares about our needs. I was confident that if God cared about giving me confirmation, then surely He cared about my other concerns, which should have left no reason to fear.

My peace I give you. I do not give to you as the world gives. Do not let your hearts be troubled and do not be afraid. (John 14:27 NIV)

Fear, however, continued to attack. My concern at this point was my husband. There was no easy way to share with Brad what I had to share. My preparation, though, needed to begin with inform-ing him of my plans. I feared how he would respond to the news I had to share. Up to this point, he hadn't seemed accepting of me con-sidering divorce and communication was stressful already between us. Revealing my plan of action was bound to add to our already stressed relationship.

Be alert and of sober mind. Your enemy the devil prowls around like a roaring lion looking for someone to devour. (1 Peter 5:8 NIV)

The devil, however, cannot keep anyone from God's plan.

In this world you will have trouble. But take heart! I have overcome the world. (John 16:33 NIV)

Keeping God's promises in mind, I mustered up what courage I had to share with Brad my intentions to file for a divorce. He was hurt like I was concerned he would be. Courage was hard to find at that moment, for conversation between Brad and I grew even more stressful.

I was tempted to give in and stay for the sake of not hurting Brad. But I believed in my spirit that wasn't the answer. I had my own well-being to consider and the well-being of my children. I needed to stand firm in what I believed to be true.

> *Stand your ground, putting on the belt of truth and the body armor of God's righteousness. (Ephesians 6:14 NLT)*

Regarding Brad, I felt within my spirit, the Lord whisper, "He is My responsibility."

> *He heals the brokenhearted and bandages their wounds. (Psalm 147:3 NLT)*

From the moment I read the poem from my son, I believed in my heart that God used him to guide me in which direction to go. I couldn't help but wonder how much longer the seemingly never ending journey that I was on would last and how everything would fall into place.

"How much longer will this last?" I asked God.

"The end is coming soon," was the response I felt within.

I wondered what was meant by "soon." Soon to God could have been another twenty years… I longed to be free that very moment— free from a place of rejection that had crushed my spirit and caused my heart such hurt for so long and free from feeling trapped in a place I didn't want to be.

"Enjoy your children," whispered a calm, soft response in my spirit.

"That's right," I told myself. My children were blessings I was careful not to take for granted. My grip on them grew tighter yet, for I believed in my heart the day was coming when their dad and I would be living separately.

While waiting for the timing to be right and enjoying my children in the present moments, reality looked me in the face. There was much preparing to do; I needed to find an attorney, a home for my children and I, and a job to provide for us… I needed strength for what was ahead. How I wished I could bypass all that needed to be done and be where I believed God planned for me to be. That was wishful thinking… I knew that arriving to my destination was going to take determination and hard work, for the devil wants nothing more than to keep God's children down and to stop His plan. The devil knows all of our weaknesses and will attempt to intervene and have control whenever he sees a child of God moving toward his or her goal.

If I was going to fulfill my destiny, it was necessary for me to turn my back on the enemy and declare, "No more!" Instead of clinging to fear, wishing my struggles would fade, I needed to shake off what was holding me back and step up like the donkey did in the fable, *Donkey in the Well,* by an unknown author. With every shovel of dirt that was thrown on the donkey, the donkey shook it off and took a step up until he reached to the top, stepped over the edge of the well, and trotted off.

I prayed for endurance to continue my journey, for courage to do what was needed, for faith in God to provide, and for hope not to be stolen. I committed to embracing my struggle to become who God created me to be and live the life I felt called to live and to cling to *Philippians 4:13 (BSB), "I can do all things through Christ who gives me strength."*

To help me stay committed in faith to move forward and not look back, I kept my son's poem, the angel dust, and the prayer from my dad tucked in my Bible. I continued praying to God, relying on Him to show me the way and give one sign after another to me through scripture, a song, movie, or word of encouragement from a friend.

Thanks be to God for loving me through loved ones who the Lord equipped to walk along side of me, for being faithful to answer my prayers, and for providing what I needed, when I needed it. I had my parents, close friends, and my sisters to turn to for support and encouragement. They helped me during my moments of weakness when I doubted or felt afraid. And there was my son, so young, but my inspiration to keep me believing and moving forward. He confidently assured me, "God will provide," when I shared with him my concerns about what kind of house and job I'd find to provide for us. His confidence gave me hope that all would be well, for I believed it was so that God cared about us.

> *Do not be afraid, for I have ransomed you.*
> *I have called you by name; you are mine. (Isaiah*
> *43:1 NLT)*

Out of the blue, while working in the yard one day that spring, the lyrics from the song, "Moving On," by Rascal Flatts played in my thoughts. It's a song about finding strength in moments of weakness after having dealt with the enemy, and having peace within about moving on from a place of blame and feeling trapped in exchange for forgiveness and a life that has been patiently waiting. Feeling moved by the song and appreciative of God's goodness, grace, and mercy, I thanked Him for healing me and for being my friend.

I was convinced that God was letting me know through the reminder of that song that the time was drawing near for me to move on. Feeling confident, my next step was to contact an attorney and prepare questions and concerns to discuss. My biggest concern was getting full custody of my children rather than joint; even one night apart would have been difficult for my children and me—several in a row surely may have been too much to bear.

My sister, Mary, was with me for much needed support the day I met with my attorney. I recall how frightened I was that I'd be told there's a good chance I'd have to share custody with my soon-to-be ex-husband; my heart pounded with sheer terror. My attorney reassured me there was no reason for concern. I prayed that would be the case and planned to serve divorce papers to Brad within the next couple of months and move out at the end of the next hunting season, which was six months away.

> *Fear not, for I am with you; be not dismayed,*
> *for I am your God; I will strengthen you, I will*

help you, I will uphold you with my righteous right
hand. (Isaiah 41:10 ESV)

I then began my search for a home for my children and me to
live. That step started off with an unexpected disappointment. My
plan was to find ourselves a house in our hometown for the sake of
being close to my children's father as well as to my family. Since I
wasn't financially set, I planned to rent a house instead of having to
purchase.

My mom, dad, and I looked at the few houses that were available in town. None of them were for rent; what was available wasn't
worth purchasing. I got a sinking feeling in my heart that perhaps I
was supposed to stay where I was and settle for what I had instead of
moving on.

Several days later, a modest house within budget was for sale that
my dad and my brother, Cory, planned to purchase. I was grateful for
their willingness to help and excited to find a home, but learned that
the house had sold a moment before my dad made the phone call
to discuss the purchase. It appeared nothing suitable was available
in my hometown where I wanted to start my new beginning. My
friend, Karen, reminded me of her advice that often an easy fix may
not be God's plan. She reassured me that God had a different plan
and I needed to be patient and keep my trust in Him. I shared with
Eric that the home God may provide to live in could end up being a
run-down house. Eric didn't seem concerned.

Fear can be a trap, but if you trust in the
LORD, you will be safe. (Proverbs 29:25 ERV)

My birthday was coming up and Eric asked to go with me to
the Hallmark store. He showed me a prayer box he wanted to buy
for me…how thoughtful. I gave him money to buy it. He said I can
write prayers to God and keep them safe in the box…that's what I
did! I wrote a prayer to God and asked for a home and job suitable
for the needs of my children and me. I prayed also for the custody

battle to go in my favor and for what suffering may be necessary to endure during the storm to be placed upon me and not my children.

When Mother's Day arrived, Eric wrapped a window hanging that he said his dad let him pick out with the words, "May all your dreams come true" on it. He handed it to me with the biggest grin on his face as though it warmed his heart as much to give as it warmed mine to receive. Jenna was a little tot then, just four, but able to sign her name to the card her brother picked from both of them. For me, being a mom was the most rewarding experience ever. I truly felt like the luckiest mom.

> *Children ae a gift from the Lord; they are a*
> *reward from him. (Psalm 127:3 NLT)*

Spring came to a close and I hadn't yet found a home for my children and me nor had I come upon an opportunity for a job. I was nervous about the status of both, but again, Eric didn't seem to be. He assured me that God will come through for us and provide.

Suddenly, that summer, I was notified that the teacher's assistant position for the preschool where I had been volunteering my time was available. I applied for the position and was hired! No more than two weeks later, I was approached by the owner of the local bank in town and was offered a job to clean the bank during the week at my convenience. The owner actually came out of the bank to approach me as I was walking by. *What a blessing!* I thought. God provided two very ideal jobs just like my son reassured me He would! Not only that, after word got out that I cleaned the bank, I was asked by several people in town to clean their house for them as well, which fit into my schedule on the days off from preschool. God is good and faithful to keep His promises!

School started back up. Eric turned ten years old over the summer and was in the fourth grade. Jenna turned five and was in her last year of preschool where I was now employed. I was thankful for being provided with jobs that fit perfectly for a single mom, which I was about to be.

My final hunting season was upon me, the seventh one. I served Brad divorce papers at the start of the season, fourteen years after being married. I shared with him that I would move out after our last client was served. Not a word was spoken or argument started about the arrangement I requested. I was nervous though, for I still hadn't found a home.

After a week into the hunting season, I was walking past the bank where I had been employed and happened to be drawn to go inside. Given no reason other than believing God must have prompted me, I honored the nudge and went inside.

The loan officer was available, so I stepped into his office and shared that I filed for a divorce and planned to move out in less than two months, but hadn't yet found a home. I inquired about a loan to purchase a trailer house, but wasn't financially set to take out a loan either. The loan officer suggested instead that I visit with his friend, Roger, who was a practicing doctor in another state who had a house in town where he stayed only on occasion. Roger just happened to be back for hunting at the time and was leaving for home the following morning. *What a coincidence*, I thought.

I met with Roger that evening. He offered his home rent free to my children and me. He shared that his friend from the bank, whom I visited with, told him I came from a good family and would do a fine job keeping up his house in exchange for living there during a difficult time in my life. What had happened was no coincidence. It was God's perfect and divine timing… His hand of provision and His favor on the lives of my children and me!

Yes, you came when I called; you told me, "Do not fear." (Lamentations 3:57 NLT)

I was taken aback by the goodness of our Lord and His provision. He provided far more than I imagined He would with not just a "so-so, get by" job and home but jobs that I enjoyed and wouldn't have to leave my children behind. He also provided a big, beautiful, completely furnished, brick home with two fireplaces, a family room, three bathrooms, four bedrooms, a heated garage, two patios, and a big yard with trees. Eric smiled a big grin as though to say, "I told you God would come through!"

I realized that God closed the door on me when I wanted to rent a house and on my dad and my brother when they wanted to purchase one for me, not because He didn't care or because it was His will for me to stay where I was, but because He had a better plan. Not only did God provide a beautiful house with a spacious yard for my children and me to enjoy, but also a neighbor that oversaw the yard and home. The Lord loved my children and me and cared too much to give us anything less than what He knew was best. Praise God!

> *For the LORD is good. His unfailing love continues forever, and his faithfulness continues to each generation. (Psalm 100:5 NLT)*

In what spare time I had over the next couple of months between my jobs and the hunting business, I prepared what would be home for my children and me by washing and painting the walls, cleaning out the cabinets, and packing up belongings of my children and mine. My heart was filled with such thankfulness for God's mercy and grace. My attitude was positive for what was to come. Even the tension between Brad and me quieted. I trusted God's favor would continue to reign over my life and the lives of my children. I trusted God's care over Brad as well.

Our home was cleaned and ready to move into by the end of the hunting season…right on time.

> *Be anxious for nothing, but in everything by prayer and supplication, with thanksgiving, let your requests be made known to God; and the peace of God, which surpasses all understanding, will guard your hearts and minds through Christ Jesus. (Philippians 4:6–8 NKJV)*

POINTS TO PONDER

What challenge in your life are you worrying about that God already has the solution to?

Do you continue to feel unworthy of receiving a desire you believe God has put in your heart?

Are you waiting on confirmation from God that you're headed in the right direction?

Perhaps what you desire looks to be impossible and you don't see any way it could ever be granted. Perhaps you're still trying to figure out on your own how to have what you desire. Or perhaps while waiting, you've received "No" for an answer to something you were expecting would be a "Yes."

Perhaps you're even second guessing what you thought you were supposed to do because God suddenly became silent or it's taking longer than you expected.

Perhaps you're frightened of what the outcome will be and you're tempted to settle.

Fear and doubt will try to talk you out of God's call on your life, dear one. The devil knows your weaknesses and will use them in his plan to keep you from your calling. He does not attack because you are weak like you may think. He attacks because you are growing closer to your God-given dreams and to our Lord. The closer you draw near, the harder the devil will work against you and try to separate you from our Lord. God is in control though. Not only does He know where you've been, but also where you are going. He already has the solution before you had the problem. When we attempt to figure out a plan on our own, however, we can easily fall for the devil's lies and tricks as well as attachments not of God. When we do this, we give the devil a foothold in our lives.

Cling then to God's Word. Know that when God says, "No" to something you want, it is because He has something even better. Watch for signs of confirmation that you are on the right path. The more you study God's Word, the wiser you will be to discern His voice. *John 10:27 (ESV)* says, *"My sheep hear my voice, and I know them, and they follow me."* Dare to believe even when you don't see. Trust in God's promises and perfect timing. When He makes a promise, He won't change His mind. It says so in *Hebrews 13:8 (NIV)*, *"Jesus Christ is the same yesterday and today and forever."* He won't be a second too late or too early.

Prayer: Dear God, thank You that I matter to You and that You show me Your love through the blessings You give. Thank You for the promises You put in my heart. Help me to hold tightly to them no matter how impossible they may seem. Forgive me for the times I have taken my eyes off You during a storm I have faced and attempted to make plans of my own. Thank You for giving me confirmation when I need a sign that I'm heading in the right direction, and for helping me to keep my eyes open, watching for the ways You speak to my heart. Thank You for making the impossible possible and for giving me something even better than I was expecting when Your answer is, "No." Help me to live in that place of peace, knowing that You have the solution even before I have the problem. Give me strength to embrace my struggle and to hold tight to my calling and Your Word when the devil attacks. Help me to put my trust in Your promises, to believe even when I don't see, to keep my focus on You, and to follow where You're leading me. In the name of Jesus, I pray. Amen.

Chapter 5

---❧❧❧---

GOD RESPONDS

*Call to me and I will answer you and tell you great
and unsearchable things you do not know.*

—Jeremiah 33:3 (NIV)

Several weeks before Christmas, one month short of a year from receiving my son's poem and facing what needed to be done, I turned my back on fear, packed up the last of the belongings of my children and mine in the car that my parents gave to me, and took a leap of faith for a new beginning. With my parents' help, my children and I got settled in a new home for us.

For so long I feared what this day may bring, but at the same time, I couldn't wait for it to arrive. It saddened me that my now ex-husband's heart was broken. Had I stayed though, and not pressed through the fear, guilt, and doubt, I would have remained tight in a bud and never bloomed. I trusted that God had a plan, a plan that I would become all He wanted me to be, a plan that would show others the power and love of our Lord.

And the day came when the risk to remain
tight in a bud was more painful than the risk it
took to blossom. (Anais Nin)

95

Our new home felt like "home." Not just to me, but I believed to my son as well. When Eric arrived home from school the first day, his comment, "This feels like home," brought not only a smile to my heart, but validation that I made the right decision. A resting place is what our new home felt like to me…a place that felt safe, secure, and at peace, a place to be still, to rest a while, and to discover the "me" God made me to be.

After our evening meal, my children and I took a stroll to the bank to clean it. I felt God's presence under the December sky beaming with millions of stars that shined on the snow-covered ground while Eric and I took turns pulling Jenna on the sled. The air was cold, but still, I felt blessed in that moment and certain that God's hand of provision was upon us.

When my children and I returned from cleaning the bank, we sat on the couch enjoying the peaceful surroundings and counted our blessings. Eric shared that it felt good to see me happy. It felt good to me too. I was at peace with a calm heart; to start anew and look forward to a new chapter that had begun and all that God had planned for our lives.

The following day was a new day, and with every new day comes new experiences.

It was Friday, the first visit for my children and their dad. The custody battle went in my favor which meant the arrangement was set up for Eric and Jenna to visit their dad twice a week for a couple of hours and to have one overnight a weekend with him. I believed the transition of one overnight a weekend verses an entire weekend every other week would be easier for my children.

Since it was the weekend, it was planned that Eric and Jenna would spend an overnight that Friday with Brad. I was certain this wasn't going to be easy for them…or for me, but I counted my blessings believing this arrangement outweighed joint custody, equal time for both Brad and me, which was common for divorced couples.

I drove my children to their dad's house early that evening and hung out with them until Brad arrived home from work. While we waited, they colored a picture for their dad to hang on the wall. While they colored, I reassured them that they'd come back home to me in the morning when their dad went to work and that we'd plan a fun day together. I encouraged them to help their dad prepare supper and to cuddle him if either of them or their dad felt sad.

I dreaded Brad's arrival, for I knew it would be difficult leaving my children behind. I worried how they'd get through the night without me. Aside from the one night away from Eric for the birth of Jenna, I had always been there... We were inseparable.

My stomach was in knots, not so much for me as for my children, more so for Jenna, five and a half years old, who may have been too young to comprehend what was happening at the time. Eric, on the other hand, seemed to have an unusual understanding, wisdom, and strength for his age, ten and a half years old. His faith in God to provide was incredible. I believed it was because God knew Jenna and I would need him to lean on; therefore, God made him strong and tuned in to the Lord. My son, it seemed, was the glue God used to hold us together.

> *Before I formed you in the womb I knew you,*
> *before you were born I set you apart. (Jeremiah 1:5*
> *NIV)*

My nerves shake to this day when I look back on that night... the memory of it still makes me tear up. I tried hard not to let my feelings show when I hugged my children goodbye and goodnight that evening after their dad arrived home. I couldn't let them see me fall apart, not at that moment. Nor could I look back, for they may have seen pain in my eyes that surely would have caused them an even greater hurt. I didn't want it to be any more difficult for them than what it already may have been.

I cried on my way out the door and all the way back to our new home praying for strength for my children and me that night and for God to comfort us, mostly my children. I needed reassurance desperately that all would be well, but the one who I counted on most for reassurance wasn't there. *Who would have thought my little boy would have been such a comfort and inspiration to me? Who would have thought I would have grown so connected to my children?* It was me who questioned when I first became pregnant if I could handle a baby of my own to care for every day. As it turned out, my children were what I lived for. After becoming a mom, I discovered that what I used to think mattered didn't matter anymore, and what I thought wouldn't matter, ended up mattering more than I ever thought.

During that heart-wrenching moment on my drive back home and the uncertainty of what my children were experiencing, I questioned if my desire for what I believed God had in store for us was worth the pain my children and I would suffer. At an early age, I believed so strongly in my heart that I would be happily married, have children of my own, and play a special role in helping the hurting by giving them reason for hope. I believed that was my calling, my purpose—what God had planned for my life.

Prior to the difficulty of having to leave my children behind, I believed and accepted there was a purpose for the pain in my struggling marriage, the purpose being that God would use me to help others that would go through a similar struggle as mine. Now that I was one step closer to what I believed was my calling and was faced with the hardest part of the test, parting from my children, I wasn't sure I could do what I thought God wanted me to do. Walking away without my children felt unbearable… I needed every bit of strength to help me through that moment…to help me through that night. I called out to God for assurance that there was purpose for the pain even in that most difficult moment.

He will listen to the prayers of the destitute.
He will not reject their pleas. (Psalm 102:17 NLT)

Perhaps you are in the middle of a storm, a storm similar to mine in which you believe God has given direction, but you've reached the most painful, frightening part of being obedient to God, and like me, you wonder if you can continue.

Cast all your anxiety on him because he cares
for you. (1 Peter 5:7 NIV)

I couldn't go to my mom and dad for encouragement or comfort that night. They couldn't see me hurt the way I was. It would have caused them such pain. Instead, I felt called to go to my friend, Karen, the one who said God's plans often aren't easy. She offered comfort during my moment of suffering that God was present in my circumstance, that He wouldn't leave my children and me, and that even that most painful moment had purpose. She shared that moving forward means having to make adjustments we won't always find comfortable, but that God promises to walk with us.

> *Be strong and courageous. Do not be afraid*
> *or terrified because of them, for the LORD your God*
> *goes with you; he will never leave you nor forsake*
> *you. (Deuteronomy 31:6 NIV)*

There's a saying, "If God brings you to it, He will help you through it." It most certainly was agonizing going through that experience and thinking about what my children were going through. I believed Karen though, that God was right there with me and with my children. I found strength and encouragement in her words to press forward. I found comfort also in the words from my son's poem that God would be there to help us through the storm. Perhaps God gave my son the title to his poem, "Don't Look Back," because it was of essence that I do not look back at that most difficult moment when I said goodbye to my children. It was of essence, too, that I trust God during this time and keep my focus on His faithfulness instead of on the storm.

> *Whoever dwells in the shelter of the Most High*
> *will rest in the shadow of the Almighty. I will say of*
> *the LORD, "He is my refuge and my fortress, my*
> *God, in whom I trust." (Psalm 91:1–2 NIV)*

After arriving home that evening, I put my trust in the Lord that He would help my children and I through the night and I quieted my heart. I turned on some music and gave our home a welcoming touch by organizing the rooms and hanging photos on the walls late into the night.

The doorbell rang early in the morning at the arrival of my son and daughter. I ran to greet them with hugs and kisses. Within minutes, my happiness turned to heartbreak, for I learned from Eric that the night ended up being more difficult than I expected for him and his sister without me. Jenna was sad and hid herself under the bed at her dad's house to cry. She must have been so frightened, worried, and confused about what was happening…she had never spent a night apart from me. I imagined how scared and sad she may have felt. I recalled a time I was without my mom when she needed surgery and had to stay in the hospital when I was a young girl… I missed my mom terribly and cried, too, for her.

Eric shared that he and his dad tried coaxing his sister out from under the bed in which they were finally able. I don't know what kept Eric from picking up the phone to call and ask me to come back like his sister, and perhaps even his dad, may so desperately have wanted. God gave my son the strength and wisdom I suppose to keep from calling, for He knew how the ending of our circumstance would turn out.

Had Eric called, there's no way I could have ignored the pain of my child or the plea of my daughter's cry for me in the background. My heart broke the moment I sensed the slightest hurt in my children. Without a doubt, I would have run to Jenna's side and bore the pain to comfort her heart.

My act of leaving wasn't done out of selfishness or just for my own good. It was for the well-being of all of us, my son, my daughter, my ex-husband, and me. I prayed long and hard about living out God's will prior to making my decision to leave and believed the outcome would draw each of us closer to the Lord as well as to our calling.

Heartbroken as I was knowing it had been a difficult night for my children, a peace came over me that the worst was behind, that what mattered was my children were back and it was a new day. I prayed that the worst indeed had passed and reminded myself that

God was faithful to answer in the past and would be faithful today and tomorrow.

> *And I am sure of this, that he who began a*
> *good work in you will bring it to completion at the*
> *day of Jesus Christ. (Philippians 1:6 ESV)*

My children and I spent the afternoon shopping for Christmas in a nearby town. It cheered my spirits and took my mind off the previous day… I hoped it did the same for Eric and Jenna.

The following week, my children and I got more into a routine. We walked a couple blocks to and from school and the preschool, together with Eric's friend, Kendra, the girl from his class and my daycare, as well as the boy next door, Brian, from Jenna's preschool. After school, while they all played, I cleaned the bank. When finished, my children and I had supper together, shared about our day, and worked on homework if need be before cuddling in bed with a story and our prayers. Living in town was an adjustment for us as we missed being in the country, but our community was pleasant and we had each other.

When the weekend arrived, I suggested to Eric and Jenna that we bake Christmas cookies with their dad at his house to help with their overnight on Saturday. They agreed. It ended up being a more relaxed and enjoyable visit for both. I was thankful and promised God I'd do what it would take for the sake of my children.

I planned Christmas Eve for them and their dad and I to celebrate together with an evening meal, the church service, and opening presents. Spending the holiday together as a family seemed it would be more enjoyable for Eric and Jenna rather than them having to be separated from either their dad or me for the holiday. It felt right in my heart to do what we did.

In the months that followed, we spent a lot of time together as a family which many criticized, but it wasn't them I aimed to please and they didn't know the promise I made to God, or the promise I made to my son to be kind to his dad. So I went about doing for my family what I believed God wanted.

> *Obviously, I'm not trying to win the approval of people, but of God. If pleasing people were my goal, I would not be Christ's servant. (Galatians 1:10 NLT)*

It was the little acts of kindness that Brad and I did for the sake of our children that I believed helped all of us get through the changes we were going through. Spending time as a family, in my eyes, demonstrated an act of love and showed our children that their dad and I cared about them and each other. It may have been the reason Brad brought Jenna back to me when she missed me during her once-a-week overnight with him. I was appreciative of his act of kindness for the sake of Jenna.

> Every act of kindness benefits the giver, as well as the receiver. (Jack Kerouac)

After several months of being in our home, Eric shared that he felt there was a "knowing" of some sort within him that there'd come a day his dad and I wouldn't be together. He said this frightened him, but when it happened, things seemed to fall into place. He shared that the experience seemed to strengthen his faith because he saw God provide for us. I too had a "knowing" of some sort that my marriage wouldn't last like I had planned. I was as scared as could be thinking about it; but, like my son, aside from the first night of being away from my children, I found letting go and moving on to be a smoother process than I ever thought possible.

> *You of little faith, Jesus replied, "Why are you so afraid?" Then He got up and rebuked the winds and the sea, and it was perfectly calm. (Matthew 8:26 BSB)*

It was no coincidence that the storm my children and I faced calmed and went as smoothly as it did. Nor was there question that favor was indeed upon my children and me. God cared about every detail in our lives and provided just like it is promised in *Matthew 6:26 (NIV)*, *"Look at the birds of the air; they do not sow or reap or store away in barns, and yet your heavenly Father feeds them. Are you not much more valuable than they?"* We witnessed His goodness, grace, and mercy in our circumstance in which our faith was made strong, and good was attained as promised in *Genesis 50:20 (NLT)*, *"You intended to harm me, but God intended it all for good."*

Feeling inspired about all God had done for us, I suggested to my children that we make prints of our feet and use them to make a wall hanging with the poem, *Footprints,* by an unknown author, on it, with sand and seashells. I recalled the poem from when I was young, but never related to its meaning until this point in my life. The poem shares about a man noticing two sets of footprints during scenes in his life in a dream, one belonging to him and the other to the Lord. He also noticed there were times when there was only one set of footprints and that it happened during his lowest, saddest times in his life. When the man questioned the Lord about the one set of footprints during his most difficult moments, the Lord responded that it was then that He carried him. It's a poem that serves as a reminder for me that God carries us through our struggles.

My devotion after completing our craft, from *The Word Among Us,* was titled, "Comfort from the Shepherd," with *Psalm 23:4 (NKJV)* *"Yea, though I walk through the valley of the shadow of death, I will fear no evil; For You are with me; Your rod and Your staff, they comfort me."* The writer described that as a child of God we are never alone, for our Shepherd is with us at all times and comforts and protects us. He explained that there are times when our Shepherd knows that the only way to get us where He wants to take us is to lead us down the path that passes through the dark valley instead of around as we might wish. Yet He walks closely with us during those times reassuring us throughout the journey that He is with us and still loves us. It is during those times, the writer explained, that we experience God's love and compassion in a deeper dimension than we ever had before. We can place our absolute trust in the Lord, our Shepherd, and know that He will protect us and show His love for us through our darkest valley. He is always prepared and knows exactly when and where we will experience difficulty, for evil never catches our Lord by surprise.

I didn't see it at the beginning of the storm, but when it was over, I looked back and saw how Jesus was there during the whole time. Undoubtedly, He carried me, along with my children, through the storm, even while I was trying to find solutions on my own, thinking God didn't care and wasn't listening. He allowed me to go through what the devil intended for harm, the storm, I believe, because He knew that's the only way He would get my attention to rely on Him. I became thankful for my struggle; it is what built my trust and relationship with the Lord. Had I not gone through it, I wouldn't have become the person that I became. Because of it, I was stronger, wiser, and confident of God's love.

I prayed Brad would experience God's favor as well. After our divorce, he expressed that he didn't know how to show his love as a husband for me. I truly believed him. Whether he was shown or not, I don't know. He became a changed man, however, the kind of man I prayed he would be while we were married, the kind of man his children needed him to be. He demonstrated a kindness toward me that made me feel valued and appreciated. In fact, I looked to him as a friend, enjoyed carrying on conversation with him, and doing activities together with our children. Eric and Jenna were blessed to witness the example of love their dad and I had developed for each other.

> *My troubles turned out all for the best—they forced me to learn from your textbook. (Psalm 119:71 MSG)*

In the spring of the year, I noticed a certain scent that randomly appeared in our home. It was the same smell I recalled while cleaning and preparing our home to move into. The scent wasn't necessarily pleasant, nor was it unpleasant. What it did was take me back to the joy and hope I felt while preparing our home for a new beginning. This left me with a feeling of gratitude for what God did and gave to my children and me. Peace settled in my heart. I praised God for all He did and gave. To make the unusual scent even more gratifying, Eric also noticed it and asked if I recognized it from when we moved into our home. It was like God sending a reminder to us of His goodness through a familiar scent.

With spring, another school year came to a close, the weather got warmer and my children and I spent more time outside. Often, Eric and Jenna's friends joined us for walks, bike rides, or play at the park. I liked having their friends over. They became like family to me. Sometimes they visited even when Eric and Jenna were visiting at their dad's house. The neighbor boy, Brian, in particular, enjoyed visiting whether my children were home or not. He suggested one afternoon that he and I have lunch together on the patio. After helping me prepare our lunch, he was polite to open the door and say, "After you," to me. Often, we'd find him waiting patiently for us on our porch steps or at the kitchen table until we arrived back home. He added smiles to our days and laughter in our hearts.

That spring, Eric suggested that I do something fun for myself while he and his sister visited their dad, like go out on a date. He had become such a caregiver, always making sure to look after his sister and me. He was protective, caring, and loving. I couldn't have asked for better. I appreciated his thoughtfulness for me to do something enjoyable for myself, but surprisingly, when he and his sister visited their dad, I enjoyed the quiet. It allowed me time to write which was a passion of mine, a help to discovering who I was and what I wanted. I enjoyed long bubble baths the one night a week that I was alone, journaling, and getting to sew, which is a skill I learned from my mom when I was a young girl.

I wasn't one who needed much for entertainment outside the home anyway, nor was I looking for a relationship at the time. My heart still reminisced with the happiness it found several years back toward Michael. I thought about him often and wondered if our paths would ever meet again. He seemed to me a Godsend—sent timely by God.

> Some people come into our lives and quickly go. Some stay for a while, leave footprints on our hearts, and we are never, ever the same. (Flavia Weedn)

If I wanted to do something while my children were with their dad, I had my neighbor lady, Julie, to visit whom I had gotten close with. I also had siblings and my parents to visit. Really, I was at peace and happy with what was. Plus, I wanted to be available for Jenna if she needed to come back home, which was sometimes the case.

One morning that spring, I woke to a whisper within, "You have been patient. Soon you will have everything you wanted... everything you hoped for. Now get up and get going."

Inspired because I believed God spoke to me like He did to Abram, Jonah, Moses, Noah, and many others in the Bible, I got myself out of bed anticipating good to come.

> *Let me hear of your unfailing love each morn-*
> *ing, for I am trusting you. Show me where to walk,*
> *for I give myself to you. (Psalm 143:8 NLT)*

The message sparked hope into my spirit that one day I'd truly have all that I dreamed of having, for *Hebrews 6:18 (NIV)* says, *"It is impossible for God to lie."* Feeling encouraged, I daydreamed about all that I wanted. Then, leaving nothing out, I boldly went to God and asked for it. I prayed that if I never crossed paths again with Michael, a man like him would come into my life and true love would be mine. I prayed for continued health and a long life for my parents, to forever remain close with my children, and that I would live a fulfilled life living out God's plan for me. I believed, for *1 John 5:14 (ESV)* declares, *"And this is the confidence that we have toward him, that if we ask anything according to his will he hears us."*

I told my sister, Loretta, about the message I received. She shared that "soon" could be twenty years or more from that time, such as it was for the promise to be fulfilled that God made to Abram that he would become the father of many nations through his own son. *That's a long time*, I thought, *but if it takes twenty years until I live the life I believe God is calling me to live, the wait will be worth it.*

> *And let us not grow weary of doing good, for*
> *in due season we will reap, if we do not give up.*
> *(Galatians 6:9 ESV)*

I asked a priest I visited with how I could know for certain that something was from God. He shared the *Saint Therese Novena: "Saint Therese, the little flower, please pick me a rose from the heavenly garden, send it to me with a message of love. Ask God to grant me the favor I thee implore and tell Him I will love Him each day more and more. Amen."* It was a Novena I was familiar with from my mom's teaching. The priest told me to watch for a sign of a rose to appear on the fifth day if indeed my prayer was in line with God's will.

Wanting to know if the desire my heart had for Michael was from God, I prayed the Novena. Upon realizing the fifth day of the Novena would land on my niece, Sarah's wedding in which I was a bridesmaid, I told myself a rose in my bouquet wouldn't count, for there were sure to be roses in the arrangements.

I arrived early to the church the day of Sarah's wedding. My heart took a fall when I was given my bouquet without a single rose. There would have been uncertainty, of course, had there been roses in it like I thought there would be, but not one rose in my bouquet, in the bride's bouquet, or even in the whole church appeared to be a straight up "No" in answer to my question.

I sulked in disbelief. I was certain my feelings for Michael were of God's work. They felt genuine. I thought what I felt for him surely must have been what love felt like. But what I felt must have been of my own doing and not at all from God like I thought.

I was sad, very sad, and angry at myself for thinking God would have actually meant for me to grow fond of another man while I was married. How ridiculous. Not only that, Michael was out of my league. He lived far from me and had a life so different than mine. He was handsome, lived in a big city, and had a business of his own, with money to enjoy things I only dreamed of. I was an ordinary girl from a farm that lived near a small community on a tight budget.

I wandered about with the other attendants, family, and my children, reminding myself how good God has been to me. The flower girl, Stephanie, my great niece, followed where I went and dropped her basket of petals by accident at my feet. I knelt down to gather the petals and the next thing I knew, the petals fell before my feet again. I teased Stephanie and jokingly asked the third time the petals fell, "What's up with your petals?"

It appeared then that a voice within whispered, "Don't you see, they are rose petals."

My goodness…they sure were! It took three times for the white rose petals to fall before me to get my attention. Perhaps it was so that Michael was a Godsend. Stephanie returned to her mom's side and to her cousins as though her purpose of following me was complete.

I daydreamed night and day about all that I wanted. I pictured my parents and children seeing me live a happy and fulfilled life. My mom commented that I was happiest when I was with my children. She was right. I was happy when I was with my children, but I knew the reality of my children growing up and having a family of their own one day. I wanted my parents and children to see me loved and taken care of by a husband who'd honor me as his wife. I wanted this and more. I wanted to live in the countryside where my children and their children would have space to roam and grow. I wanted to travel the world with my family and share with others the glory of God!

For as he thinks in his heart, so is he. (Proverbs 23:7 NKJV)

Wanting very much for my dream of a happy marriage to come true and finding myself doubting again by questioning if God really loved me that much, I prayed the *Saint Therese Novena* several months later in hopes to receive a sign of a rose from God again.

On the fifth day of the Novena while driving to my mom and dad's house that summer morning to clean, I was reminded that it was day five. I thanked God for the sign of angel dust He gave me awhile back that I'd be blessed with a happy marriage. I told Him I'd undoubtedly believe if I was given a whole pile of roses for my sign on that fifth day.

Forgetting all about the Novena after I got started cleaning, I went outside to see what Jenna and her friend, Brian, who came with us, wanted to show me. It was a pile of yellow roses that they picked from my mom's only rose bush. "Oh no," I said, "you picked all of grandma's roses!"

Just then I heard, "You asked for a whole pile of roses," speak within my spirit.

Oh goodness, that's right, I thought.

I thanked God as I knelt down, gathered the roses, and took them inside. At first, my mom let out a sigh at the sight of her roses picked and lying on the table. But when I shared that they were a sign from my Novena, she smiled and said, "They're yours then."

I imagined how life would end up for me. I had reason to believe it would be all I hoped for as God had been so good to me already and proved His faithfulness in the past.

I enjoyed the remainder of the summer with my children and appreciated what I had while I waited for my dreams to come to pass. I appreciated our home. It was big and roomy. I enjoyed cleaning it and having the windows open for fresh air like I was used to growing up. I liked our yard with green lawn and trees to provide privacy in the back. I enjoyed sitting on my wooden swing hidden by the trees just talking with Eric and Jenna or watching them play. I appreciated having a wash line in the back yard for hanging laundry which was another fond memory of mine from home. I enjoyed having a snack under the porch in the front yard with my children and sitting there watching the rain come down or the sun peak through the clouds. I loved the peace and quiet during that season in my life and the responsibility of having children to care for and hang out with. I was thankful for the good I was given and that I was just a few miles away from my parents and siblings, so I could visit frequently. I was truly blessed and appreciative.

> Concentrate on counting your blessings
> and you'll have little time to count anything else.
> (Woodrow Kroll)

That fall our school closed and consolidated with a nearby town due to low enrollment. Eric, eleven years old, entered the fifth grade. Jenna, six years old, started kindergarten. I wasn't as bothered about her starting school as I was when Eric started. Perhaps because I was on more solid ground with less stress and was confident that there was much to look forward to, and dreams that would come true. I was confident also that Jenna was ready for school and would enjoy it like her brother.

Since the preschool where I was employed was held at our school that just closed, I was without my job. I wasn't concerned however, for I had been offered the opportunity to help operate a pheasant hunting business during the fall of the year with my landlord, Roger. I was excited for the opportunity. I was familiar with the business and well-qualified to do a good job.

With both my children in school, I developed a new routine. After walking them to meet the school bus, I read through my devotions upon returning home and enjoyed journaling how my life related to them. I looked forward to that time each day between God and me, when I developed a deeper relationship with Him, a stronger passion for writing, and a desire to teach the lessons I learned.

I then went about my day preparing the lodge for the pheasant hunting operation Roger and I planned. The lodge needed painting and fixing up. It was located just a couple of miles out of town where my heart resonated with the peace and quiet in the country. My heart was content and my spirits were high; my hope was in my Lord.

> *And so, Lord, where do I put my hope? My*
> *only hope is in you. (Psalm 39:7 NLT)*

POINTS TO PONDER

Has God given you a sign or spoken a word to you that all will be well?

Perhaps the enemy has brought a storm upon your life with the intent to harm you.

Is a prayer of yours in the process of being answered, but the most difficult part of the test seems unbearable?

Perhaps, like me, you doubt if what you've been praying for is worth the pain you're experiencing.

When God calls you to do something, dear one, or is about to bless you, it's likely that fear will be present. The enemy will speak lies into you and try his best to hold you back when you are headed in the right direction. Trust, however, that God cares about every detail in your life; that He knows what is best, will be faithful to comfort you in the pain you are going through, and provide for all of your needs.

The enemy may have brought a storm upon your life to kill, steal, and destroy, but God will use it to grow you stronger, wiser, and more confident in His love for you. You may not see it now, my friend, but your most difficult season can become your most gratifying season. Where you put your faith will determine the outcome of where you end up. For when you know truth, you can put your hope in the One who speaks it and you can resist the enemy.

In God's hands intended evil becomes eventual good. (Max Lucado)

Prayer: Dear Lord, thank You that You respond to my prayers and walk with me every step of the way. Thank You that what the enemy intends for harm You use to bless me and to grow me into who You want me to be. Thank You that You are good and all-knowing; You knew me even before I was born and everything that I would be. Forgive me, Jesus, for the times I've allowed doubt to interfere with Your plan for my life. Help me to hold tight to the promises You have made even when the temptation arises to look back or give up. Surround me with others who will support the calling on my life. Help me to enjoy where I am and to appreciate the blessings You have given while I wait for the prayers in my heart to be answered. In the name of Jesus, I pray. Amen.

Chapter 6

LISTEN

*In the morning, LORD, you hear my voice; in the morning
I lay my requests before you and wait expectantly.*

—Psalm 5:3 (NIV)

As it turned out, kindergarten wasn't as enjoyable for Jenna as I thought it would be. She was outgoing and had a variety of friends she enjoyed, but being apart from me during school and again on the weekend for an overnight may have been too much at the time.

It saddened my heart to know my daughter was sad. To help her through her struggle, I visited her classroom and playground frequently and taped a photo of her and me hugging each other to her school folder so she could be reminded that we had each other. Above all, I continued to pray for her as I did for my son; I could imagine effects that divorce can have on a child. I prayed for God to continue His blessings on my family, to provide for all our needs, and give us strength to carry us through any storm that may arise from challenges yet to come.

*Do not be anxious about anything, but in
everything by prayer and supplication with thanks-*

giving, let your requests be made known to God.
(Philippians 4:6 ESV)

I taught Jenna religious education like I did for Eric. One of the teachings Jenna questioned was if God answers our prayers, why then didn't He answer her dad's prayer to bring me back. I explained that God knows what's best and answers every prayer, either with a "yes" "no" or "wait." If God says, "No," it is because He has something better for us. If God says, "Wait," it is because we are not yet ready to receive what we are asking for or all the pieces haven't yet fallen into place for the request to be fulfilled. I told Jenna God loves us too much to give us any less than what He knows is best. Eric described it well when he said his dad was a good person and I was a good person, but we may not have become what God intended us to be had we remained a couple. Comprehending what Eric and I explained, Jenna expressed an understanding.

"For I know the plans I have for you," declares
the LORD, "plans to prosper you and not to harm
you, plans to give you hope and a future." (Jeremiah
29:11 NIV)

The first hunting season for Roger and me arrived and went well. Roger guided the hunters in the fields. My job was to accommodate the hunters with breakfast and an evening meal that I prepared and served in our home. I provided, as well, a clean room for them to sleep at the farmhouse we remodeled for a lodge.

When the season ended, it was nice to get back to a quieter routine with Eric and Jenna and enjoy their Christmas break from school with them as well as Christmas traditions.

Kids spell love T-I-M-E. (John Crudele)

My favorite time, the spring of the year, arrived. The grass, the trees, and the flowers came back to life. The weather warmed up and my children were out of school for summer break! We biked and took walks in the evenings with friends and hung out at the school or the park to swing, play basketball, and roller-skate until it got dark. Life was simple in our small hometown, and it was safe. I was certainly thankful for the simple, carefree days of raising my children in a small community with friends, people we knew, and family nearby.

I continued to join my children during many of their visits with their dad. Jenna had grown stronger and better able to make it through her visit at her dad's house, though she shared through notes she wrote for me and through conversations between us that sometimes it was still a struggle being apart. I still believed, however, that the decision I made to file for a divorce was best for all of us. There wasn't a day that I didn't give our circumstance to our Lord through prayer.

> *Cast all your anxiety on him because he cares for you. (1 Peter 5:7 NIV)*

When school started back up, Eric was twelve years old, entered sixth grade, and was of age to participate in school sports and band. He participated in basketball, football, and track, along with the shooting sports he had been involved with since the age of five and also playing the drums. I wasn't much for watching sports, but I sure enjoyed watching my son play sports which he was good at, and interacting with fellow teammates who appeared to like him.

Jenna was seven years old and in the first grade. She enjoyed her second year of school significantly more than she did her kindergarten year. Like her brother, Jenna had the kind of personality that drew others to her. I was fortunate that my children were easily accepted and well liked. I was thankful for the strength from our Lord in both Eric and Jenna's spirit.

Shortly after the school year started, my second year of the hunting operation I managed got on its way. I met Robert, a hunter who asked if he could return when the season was over to take me on a date. I hadn't yet had an interest to get involved in a relationship with a man. I was focused on my children and still had Michael on my heart. Robert, however, seemed very pleasant during his stay and my children approved, so I accepted his invitation to a Christian Christmas concert the following Sunday at a nearby town.

It felt awkward being on a date. I was used to hanging out with my children and their friends and acting silly. Hanging out with Eric and Jenna felt more comfortable than being on a date. All in all though, the conversation with Robert went well. I learned he sang in the church choir. He came across as a fine Christian man.

Soon after, Robert called and asked if he could take me out for supper and dancing. I had always enjoyed dancing. I learned it from my mom when I was young and enjoyed going to dances growing up. It had been a while since I had been to a dance. I accepted and had an enjoyable time.

I was flattered over the compliments from Robert on my appearance and the praise for being the mom he saw me as to my children. I liked the way he treated me and that he showed concern for my children by telling me he understood that they come first. Still, I wasn't interested in committing myself to a relationship with a man.

After six months of accepting dates with Robert, he proposed to me. I felt an uneasiness in my spirit. I envisioned my children loving the man I'd marry and being happy when I found him. My children barely knew Robert. I barely knew him. I declined his proposal, expressing that things were happening too fast… I needed time to discern what God wanted me to do.

When I prayed for an answer, "You're settling," is the response that came to my heart about marrying Robert. I promised my heart I wouldn't settle again. With that being said, I called the relationship off; there was no sense in leading Robert on.

He seemed hurt and I was to blame. I knew very well how badly a heart can ache when it's been rejected. A weight of guilt was laid upon my shoulders for hurting another, so much that I convinced myself that I didn't give Robert, who seemed to care about me, a fair chance. Plus, he appeared to be a nice man with good morals and Christian values. Giving into guilt, I continued seeing him, this time looking for characteristics in him that I admired. Perhaps if I focused on his qualities, my feelings about being involved in a relationship with him would change.

Another school year passed. Spending time with my children remained a priority for me. They grew too quickly as it was. During that summer, I joined Julie, my neighbor lady, for a walk while my children visited their dad. She and I grew to be close friends as we talked about everything from our struggles to our joys. It was good to share my thoughts and feelings with another woman, as well as get advice, for it seemed to feel within my spirit that God was preparing me for another change. Julie's wisdom encouraged me to welcome the change that I sensed was on the way.

I still enjoyed our small community and was very thankful to live so close to family, especially my mom and dad. But something new was stirring inside of me. I sensed that my children were getting bored with what our community had to offer. Sometimes I felt that way too, but for the sake of my children and of their relationship with their dad, I kept quiet and made do... I could only imagine the pain Brad would experience if his children moved even farther away. I was willing to wait for the right time if God was calling us for a change.

As it turned out, Julie was feeling as though she was being pre-pared for a change as well. Neither of us knew what changes would take place, but we each felt a "knowing" within that a change was necessary. It was a blessing to have each other to confide in and encourage.

It was that summer that Julie introduced me to the inspirational Pastor Joel Osteen on television one evening before we went for a walk. Never before had I heard someone speak so encouraging as Joel about following one's dreams. He motivated me to listen to the dreams in my heart and to believe in them. I prayed that God would guide Julie and me in our uncertainties and dreams. I prayed that we would be given courage to move in the direction God wanted us to go and that we would grow in the process.

Perhaps you feel a stirring in your spirit that God is calling you to make a change...a change that will lead you closer to a dream in your heart. I encourage you to welcome the Holy Spirit's presence, dear one, and He will lead you where to go.

The summer passed quickly, as they all did. Eric turned thirteen years old. I could hardly believe he was already a teenager. He went into the seventh grade when school started back up and Jenna, eight years old, started second grade. Eric still thrived in playing sports and did well academically. He was gentle on the football field, thank goodness, and enjoyed the company of his teammates at practice and games.

Jenna also did well in school and thrived on entertaining friends who frequently visited at our house after school and on weekends. Her faith in God had grown stronger. She shared how she repeated Jesus' name to help her through the difficult moments when she and I were apart. She found security and comfort in my love for her. But praise God, for there's something even more special about Jesus' love and comfort!

It was a quiet hunting season for Roger and me that fall. Just a few of Roger's friends and some relatives of his were all who hunted, which left time for me to hunt with Eric on his dad's land. That was fun! I don't recall if Eric got his limit. I do recall his golden retriever, still a pup, hunted with us too, but she tuckered out and headed back to the truck where she waited for us to return.

The school year was busier than usual. I attended Eric's sport activities along with the usual music concerts, programs, and conferences for both Eric and Jenna. Between activities at school, religious education for my children, and visiting my mom and dad, our weeks were over before I knew it.

Even with the busyness, my heart still sensed a change up ahead …a change of location perhaps. Uncertain, I prayed and waited for God to guide me and prepare my children's hearts and mine if it was His will for us to make a move to relocate.

As it turned out, Eric shared his thoughts that it seemed to him we were being prepared for a change of location. Our hearts were in tune with each other's again. I shared with Eric that I had been feeling the same, but I wasn't sure how he and his sister would feel. I didn't want to take them farther from their dad.

Just days after Eric and I talked about the possibility of relocating, Roger informed me that he was retiring from the medical field. He wanted to move into his house that my children and I were welcomed to stay in for the past three years. Fortunately, he gave us until the end of the school year which was a few months to prepare.

It was so. God indeed was preparing my children and me for a change…a change where I had no say in whether to go or to stay. Our welcome was over and it was time to move in a new direction. I didn't know yet where the change would take us, but, "One step at a time," I told myself.

I thought about where I wanted to relocate. Family mattered to me, so I didn't want to go far. I didn't expect my children to be willing to move far from their dad either. After talking it over with my children, we decided on a near-by community an hour away, still close enough to make frequent visits back home to my mom and dad and Eric and Jenna's dad. The community was quite a bit larger in population, over twenty-five thousand, compare to the few hundred we were used to. We were familiar, however, with the community and comfortable with its size.

I dreaded having to share the news with Brad. He had already been hurt by the divorce; I didn't want to add to his pain. However, I knew I must share.

After sharing with Brad, I started looking into options for a job. I didn't know what I'd find for employment, for a home, or how my children would adjust to a bigger community and a more populated school. I reminded myself that God had been faithful to provide in the past and He would be faithful to provide again.

As I searched the newspaper ads for employment, I reflected on my dream to help others. I gave thought to going back to school for a degree in Counseling. After visiting the college in the community where we'd be living and sorting through ideas, it appeared the Lord spoke, "You already know what I want you to teach My children."

I took it that going back to college wasn't necessary for God's plan for me. I went back to scanning the newspaper ads for employment, attended a job fair, and began applying at several locations. I was choosy as far as hours and days for the sake of my children, but limited since I only had one year of college.

I accepted a job I was offered with hours that I was looking for in the community where we were relocating. It was with a company that did background checks for employers. I then began my search for a home for my children and me. My plan was to rent instead of making a purchase. After seeing the cost of available rental units, my dad recommended that I put my money toward the purchase of a home.

Buying a home frightened me. I didn't see how I'd be able to afford house payments along with the other bills I'd be expected to pay. I feared I was taking too big of a step. Miraculously though, I came across a program that offered an affordable price for a brand-new home. It seemed too good to be true—much like our home we moved into right after my divorce, but after looking into the program, it indeed looked as though it would be feasible.

My mom, dad, my children, and I toured the home for sale. It was a good-sized two bath, split-level home with four bedrooms, a double stall garage, and a big yard in a nice neighborhood. We all liked it! I went from doubting I could make ends meet to believing it could happen!

My next step after settling on a home was to enroll Eric and Jenna in a school in the community where we would be living. It just so happened that the school we were interested in was located within a few blocks from our home. The only recommendation was for my children and me to be living in the home by the time the next school year started at the end of the summer. It was going to be a few months until our home would be ready to move into, but we'd be moved in just in time for the deadline.

Employment started for my new job in April. The hours were Monday through Friday during the day, which fit nicely into my children's schedule at school. I commuted to and from work since our new home wasn't complete. I continued to clean the bank for extra income needed for the gas it cost to commute and for furniture and appliances for our home.

When the school year ended, my children and I packed up our belongings to move in with my mom and dad on the farm until our new home was ready. I took one last look around before saying goodbye to what had been "home" to my children and me for the past three and a half years.

It was a good home for us where wonderful memories were made: memories of playing in the yard in the leaves and in the snow with my children and their friends and hanging out with them at the school, on a bike ride, or a walk in the dark. I enjoyed the winter nights on the patio under the stars in the hot tub with Eric and Jenna, cuddling with them during a movie and at bedtime, the closeness of sharing about our day, and the overnights my children's friends spent with us.

All of what I experienced in the home and community where my children and I lived would be memories I'd hold dear. Part of me wanted to stay…but another part of me was excited for what was to come, for it seemed God had prepared the hearts of my children and me well for the change He had in store for us.

I was reminded of Abram. *Genesis 12:1–2 (NIV)* says, *"The Lord had said to Abram, 'Go from your country, your people and your father's household to the land I will show you. I will make you into a great nation, and I will bless you; I will make your name great, and you will be a blessing.'"* I knew in my heart that it was time…time to go and explore more of what my children and I were meant to experience that would draw all of us closer to our calling.

I was grateful for Roger's generosity of welcoming his home to my children and me and appreciative of the friendship he and I grew. I thanked God for the starting point to get us on our feet, for the faith that grew in us, for the peace and quiet that lived in my heart, for the memories we made as we grew, and for the good I believed that was yet to come. I then whispered goodbye to a home that was good to my children and me in so many ways, and I shut the door.

Eric, Jenna, and I spent the next three months at my mom and dad's house. Eric earned an income helping on the cattle and grain farm that summer where his dad worked and Jenna hung out with her grandparents and a friend while I was at work. Arriving home from work to my children, my parents, and a hot meal was nice.

Being home with my parents was still a comfort to me...having Eric and Jenna there made it even better.

Home is where the heart is. (Pliny the Elder)

Just in time, the weekend before school started, our home was complete. My children and I with the help of my parents packed up our belongings one more time and got settled in our new home. It was an exciting move for us!

I enjoyed being only minutes away from my job instead of an hour. I also enjoyed not having to run to a second job after working a full-time one. Jenna, nine years old and in the third grade, was ecstatic over the number of friends to choose from and the opportunity for activities in a larger community. Eric, fourteen years old and in the eighth grade was happy too, but several weeks later expressed feeling overwhelmed in a much larger school than he was used to. This concerned me. If either my son or daughter was bothered, I was too. It was Eric who always remained positive, no matter the situation. Because he felt overwhelmed, I turned to doubt and questioned if the right decision was to move away and buy a house.

I missed home too. I missed living so close to my mom and dad. I never lived more than just a few miles away from them. I was used to running to their house at any given time...whether they needed me or I needed them. With a job and a home an hour away, our visits weren't as frequent as they used to be. I also missed my more relaxed routine. I didn't enjoy working full-time outside the home. I preferred having supper in the oven by the time Eric and Jenna arrived home from school and getting to spend the rest of my evening with them like I was used to. Instead, I was having to catch up with what needed to be done after being away at my job which lessened our time and activities together.

There were other changes. The visits for Eric and Jenna with their dad went from visiting him two nights during the week and just one overnight on the weekend to one visit every Wednesday after school and most of the weekend every other week. It wasn't just Jenna who struggled with the Friday evening to Sunday afternoon visit every other week, I did too. I missed my children over the weekend. I prayed for a sign that we made the right decision and prayed for all of us to adjust.

A couple of days after Eric expressed feeling overwhelmed, he expressed a new attitude. He said it feels like he's known his new friends all his life. He shared that several weeks into our new experience it seemed too big of an adjustment, but like the first time we took a leap of faith, everything fell into place as though it was meant to be. Because he felt better, I did too.

My children and I grew more and more settled in our new home and more comfortable with our new routine. We all made new friends, mine from work and Eric and Jenna's from school. I was appreciative of our home, of being welcomed in the community, of the flexibility of my job, and that we were in a pleasant neighborhood so close to the school. I was appreciative also of our weekly rides back and forth from our new home to back home where my parents, Brad, and my siblings lived. I got to visit my mom and dad while my children visited their dad. Our drive was an hour each way, which allowed time for my children and I to get to visit and share about our day. Frequent communication with each other was something that I believed developed our relationship into what it was.

With work, school, and the activities going on for Eric and Jenna, the weeks passed quickly. Eric was involved with basketball and band through the school and Jenna joined soccer, volleyball, dance, and softball through the community. We were either driving back to our hometown for a visit or my parents and Brad were in town visiting us for activities and other occasions.

Within less than a year at my job, I grew restless with it and started looking for a new one. I had an inkling from the start of my job that I would only be there temporarily. I believed in my heart God had bigger plans for me. I believed the struggles I experienced were preparing me to teach and help others in situations such as mine.

Truthfully, I longed to be a stay-at-home mom again. I had a passion to be a writer and teach by sharing experiences and lessons I learned in hopes that many come to know our Lord and draw near to

Him as well. At the time, however, I needed a job to provide for my family. I wanted one with good hours, of course, for the sake of my family, but one that was also fulfilling. My job offered a good salary and hours that fit my schedule. However, it wasn't a good fit for my personality. It offered little communication with others and very little exercise. I was more of an "on the go…how can I help you?" type of person.

I turned to God in prayer for a more satisfying job and started looking for other opportunities and applying for what I thought might be a better fit for me. While dropping my children off at school one morning, the words, "That's where I want to work," spoke loud and clear within my spirit. The voice came so boldly and out of the blue that it made me chuckle and say, "Oh really?" I didn't pay much attention to what I heard myself announce on the inside. I had already had an interview at one of the banks in town and was confident that I did well.

It ended up I wasn't offered the job like I hoped… I sulked when I was given the news that I did well, but the job was offered to another. I continued to apply for other jobs and had another interview for a secretary position at a preschool which I felt even more confident about. I wasn't offered that job either. I felt even more let down to hear I did really well, but wasn't offered the position.

The following week, Maddie, a coworker and friend, coincidently loaned me a book by Joel Osteen, who I had been watching every Sunday evening on television for inspiration. I read through the book feeling inspired to keep praying and believing a new job was on the way. I prayed silently at my desk at work for a more fulfilling job. While on break, I circled the office building outside as I walked and prayed with expectation.

Months passed…no new job.

The first year for Eric and Jenna at a new school came to a close.

Fear worked its way into my spirit that I'd be stuck with the job I had because I lacked qualification for something better. I prayed, though, through the fear that God would come through. When I prayed, I felt a calmness in my spirit not to worry. As soon as I went about my work though, thoughts of fear and worry attacked to the point that I found myself in the vicious cycle once again of doubting, worrying, and living in fear.

I doubted I'd find time to complete a manuscript I was writing for a book I hoped to publish. I worried about continuing to get by on just one job due to the cost of living expenses. A second job, I feared, would allow even less time with Eric and Jenna.

It was then that Robert proposed to me again. In my moment of vulnerability and fear that I'd never make it on my own, I let my heart down and said, "Yes."

A piece of hope fell from my spirit the moment I responded to the proposal, for I knew my heart truly wasn't in it to marry Robert even with the attempt to give him a second chance. My stomach felt tangled in knots.

Oh my, I thought. *What did I do?*

As quickly as I asked what I just did, *What was I to do?* ran through my thoughts as I didn't see how I'd be able to provide for my children on my own.

I didn't know how I'd share the news with Eric and Jenna that I had been proposed to. They hadn't yet grown fond of Robert. Nor were they asked permission by him to marry me. Again, I asked myself what I was thinking when I said, "Yes," to the proposal. The frightening thoughts, *You won't make it alone*, ran through my mind.

The knots in my stomach grew. It was important to me that my children be happy with whom I married. Yet at the same time, it was important to me that my children were provided for. After toiling several hours with fear that I wouldn't be able to provide for much longer for the needs of Eric and Jenna with the income I made, I shared my news with them.

Neither of them were pleased. I reassured them that if it is fear they have of losing my love, they'll never lose it. I reassured them too that we'd be better off financially if I got married and I would have more time to spend with them. That wasn't what concerned them. Eric and Jenna believed we'd always be close. They believed also in their hearts that Robert wasn't the one for me. They had no fear of not being provided for. Neither did they fear that the right man wouldn't come along. They wanted to see me happy, and they believed that in due time I would be.

Who was I kidding? Had I truly been happy, my children wouldn't have needed convincing of any kind. Not only that. My thoughts repeatedly went back to Michael who I had been fond of eight years by this time. I beamed inside and out while in his presence during our encounter. It was that feeling I believed God wanted me to feel toward a companion.

Believing it would be a mistake to follow through with a wedding the following spring with Robert, I prayed for courage to do what was right. I kept silent from sharing with anyone at the time what was on my heart. I suppose so no one could hold me accountable if I couldn't bring myself to follow through with doing what I believed deep in my soul God wanted me to do...to call off the proposal I accepted and break off all ties with the man I said yes to.

I couldn't seem to tune out the frightening thoughts that providing for my family would be too difficult. Eric and Jenna didn't give up though on making me see what they saw. They shared that I wasn't the carefree, "happy-go-lucky" person they knew me to be in my fiancé's presence. I believed they were right.

While continuing to pray, it seemed a whisper from within revealed, "I have provided all along; I always will."

I pondered for a moment on what I believed God spoke... It was true, God had always provided.

> *For God hath not given us the spirit of fear;*
> *but of power, and of love, and of a sound mind. (2*
> *Timothy 1:7 KJV)*

Meanwhile, an opening became available that summer for an assistant teacher with the Head Start Program in my community. I was confident that I would be a good candidate for that position since I was employed through Head Start back home as the assistant teacher for our preschool. Incidentally, there was also a position available for a secretary position at the middle school Eric attended; the place where I surprisingly declared a few months back that I'd one day be employed. I interviewed for both positions and surprisingly was offered both.

God is good! He came through for me and answered my prayer for a better job. Why I made trusting God so difficult, I don't know.

> *Why are you cast down, O my soul, and why*
> *are you in turmoil within me? Hope in God; for I*
> *shall again praise him, my salvation and my God.*
> *(Psalm 42:11 ESV)*

I gave my two weeks' notice at my current job to accept the secretary's position at the middle school that Eric attended and Jenna would be attending.

When school started up two weeks later, Eric, fifteen years old, entered high school as a freshman and started driving himself to school. Oh my, how the time passed quickly. It seemed like just yesterday my son started kindergarten and needed help with homework and picking out his clothes; now he was driving on his own and working a job after school.

Jenna was ten years old, entered the fourth grade and had more friends than I could keep track of. She was a social butterfly on the go, into sports, and all about fun. She was mindful, however, of what made others happy. One day she and a friend came upon a garage sale in the neighborhood. She returned home with a "Dare to Dream" window decoration for me. She heard me talk plenty about my dreams and must have known I'd find inspiration from the words written on the decoration. I treasured it like the one from Eric a while back and keep both hanging in my kitchen window.

I liked my new job! I was pleased to be back in the school setting, excited that I was the secretary where Jenna would soon be attending school, and that I'd have summers off like I had been used to with my children.

Coincidently, one of the qualifications for my new job was a year of office experience. I understood why God kept me at my previous job longer than I wanted. I needed the experience to move into a better position. I realized also that God was telling me, "Wait," when I wasn't offered the other positions I had applied for. He had something better in mind. It turned out the secretary position I was offered fit my "on the go…can I help you?" personality very well! My new job offered me the opportunity to nurture and care for others, as well as I acted as the school nurse for students feeling ill.

Thank goodness God knows what's best and that He didn't allow me to have what He knew wasn't a right fit for me. I thanked Him for the new job He provided me and for answering another prayer! God is faithful!

God wasn't done with me. I had an unfinished matter in my life that needed my attention and action. Because I allowed fear to have the upper hand in making my decision about getting married, I continued to lack courage to call off my wedding. I reflected on *John 10:10 (NIV)*, *"The thief comes only to steal and kill and destroy; I have come that they may have life, and have it to the full,"* and believed God wanted happiness for my children and me. Quite sure that I wasn't supposed to marry Robert, but wanting truth revealed, I visited the church chapel after work for a week, asked God to reveal the truth, and to give me courage to do what was necessary.

Over the next several weeks, pieces of truth were revealed. Truth that would have affected our finances and trust in our relationship. Wanting to know if there was more information kept secret that would affect our relationship, I asked God if there's anything else He wanted to reveal to please do so.

Several days later while attempting to open my email, Robert's opened instead. *How strange,* I thought. His email opened without me knowing his password or even attempting to get into his mail. I was taken aback by the last of the truth revealed. What was revealed brought back painful memories from the past that would be unacceptable for my future. My son approached me to see what concerned me and then took a stand when he saw what appeared on the computer screen and insisted I call off my wedding.

For all that is secret will eventually be brought
into the open, and everything that is concealed will

be brought to light and made known to all. (Luke
8:17 NLT)

Thanks be to God for revealing truth. Thanks be to God also that my children looked out for me.

After having been assured with evidence and confirmation not to follow through with getting married, I knew what needed to be done and was ready to do it! I stood up for myself and for my children and in a rage of anger, I spoke what was on my mind as I broke off all ties once and for all with a relationship that wasn't right for me.

The LORD works righteousness and justice for
all the oppressed. (Psalm 103:6 NIV)

POINTS TO PONDER

Is there a stirring on the inside of you for a change to move closer toward your dream?

Perhaps you are tempted to please, even though your spirit senses it is not of God's will.

Perhaps God is saying, "No" to what you might think is best.

Perhaps fear is trying to convince you to settle and you are uncertain of what to do.

God is good. He will prepare you for any necessary changes, say, "No" because He loves you far too much to give less than His best, reveal truth to any uncertainties under any and all circumstances, and provide courage for you to take a stand.

Be on the lookout, my friend. The devil will disguise himself in hopes to be pleased.

And no wonder, for even Satan disguises him-
self as an angel of light. (2 Corinthians 11:14 ESV)

Prayer: Heavenly Father, thank You for caring for me and loving me the way You do to give me nothing less than the absolute best. Thank You for blessing me with loved ones who care. Help me,

Lord, to know Your voice and to listen when I am seeking truth and looking for answers. Please forgive me for the times I have failed and given into fear, for the spirit of fear does not come from You. Help me to accept when You say, "No" and trust that You know far better than me what is best. Thank You, Jesus, for revealing the truth, for guiding me in the direction You want me to go, and for giving me the courage to obey. Help me to trust You completely. I ask all this in Your precious name. Amen.

Chapter 7

—————❧—————

GOD TEACHES

Teach me your way, O LORD, that I may walk in your truth.

—Psalm 86:11 (ESV)

Whether or not my outburst of anger toward the man who proposed to me was justified, a weight was lifted from my shoulders for speaking my mind and freeing myself from a relationship I was certain I wasn't meant to continue.

Even our Lord, gentle as a lamb, roared like a lion when He cleared the temple of the moneychangers and animal-sellers in *Matthew 21:12–13 (NIV), "Jesus entered the temple courts and drove out all who were buying and selling there. He overturned the tables of the money changers and the benches of those selling doves. 'It is written,' he said to them, 'My house will be called a house of prayer, but you are making it a den of robbers.'"*

Though I was angry for being deceived, I was also angry at myself for not listening when it had been placed upon my heart that I'd be settling when I was proposed to the first time in this relationship. I was angry that I allowed myself to remain in an unhealthy relationship. I shouldn't have needed to ask for signs of what to do. Knowing Eric and Jenna were concerned and uncomfortable should have been reason enough to walk away instead of believing for changes.

I hadn't realized how hurt Eric and Jenna were because of the relationship I continued until I called off my engagement; it wasn't until then that they sincerely expressed the extent of the hurt they had been feeling. I felt terrible for causing them the hurt and concern that I did.

How I didn't see that my children were hurting the way they were, and put an end to the situation causing the pain sooner, I don't know. I must have been so caught up in the fear of financial means that I lost focus on what truly mattered—my trust in God. Instead of relying on God to provide for my children and me, I relied on false security.

Perhaps an opportunity has been presented to you. Allow me to offer a word of advice from experience. Honor and accept God's response when He says, "No," rather than falling for the trap of deception, pleasing others, or leaning on your own understanding. My friend, God knows what's up ahead. He gives us direction to show us which way to go when we ask for it.

> *Trust in the LORD with all your heart and lean not on your own understanding; in all your ways submit to him, and he will make straight your paths. (Proverbs 3:5–6 NIV)*

I asked Eric and Jenna for forgiveness, but more importantly, I asked for forgiveness from the Lord. My children forgave and were happy to put their concerns to rest. I thanked them for standing by me patiently, for loving me despite the mistakes I made, and for helping me find my way.

In the months that followed, I did my share of crying, a lot of it in my son's arms. My heart remained bitter and resentful for believing the best in another and learning the truth of who they were. I was angry for the fool I allowed myself to be and sorry for time lost with Eric and Jenna in exchange for a relationship that caused hurt. Eric listened and let me pour out my heart until he saw what anger, bitterness, resentment, and regret had done to me. He stopped me from crying by boldly making the statement, "What hurts you isn't worth the tears you cry."

Eric wasn't angry or annoyed with me. He simply cared for my well-being and knew what I held on to kept me from God's healing and His best. *Mark 11:25 (NIV)* says, *"And when you stand praying, if you hold anything against anyone, forgive them, so that your Father in heaven may forgive you your sins."*

It must have hurt my son to see me cry and know that I was hurting. His comment rang true in my heart. He knew being angry wasn't worth the life God had in store for me. God wanted to take what was hurting me and use it for good. I was thankful for Eric's compassion and words of wisdom. I admired my son's character greatly.

> You can't have a better tomorrow if you are thinking about yesterday all the time. (Charles Kettering)

I knew even if there was reason for anger, God never intended anger to control. *Ephesians 4:26–27 (NIV)* states, *"In your anger do not sin': Do not let the sun go down while you are still angry, and do not give the devil the foothold."* God doesn't want us to be resentful and bitter toward another either. *Ephesians 4:31 (ESV)* says, *"Let all bitterness and wrath and anger and clamor and slander be put away from you, along with all malice."* Lastly, God does not want us to dwell on the mistakes we made, but rather, to learn from them and move forward. *"Forget the former things; do not dwell on the past. See, I am doing a new thing"* (Isaiah 43:18–19a NIV).

Forgiving wasn't something that came easy for me. To me, saying, "I forgive you" to someone who wronged me was like saying, "What you did was okay, and you can do it again." But what we do or don't do unto others, we do or don't do unto to God. For me to be bitter and resentful toward another was to be bitter and resentful toward God. *"He will reply, 'Truly I tell you, whatever you did not do for one of the least of these, you did not do for me'"* (Matthew 25:45 NIV).

I knew if I continued dwelling on and feeding anger, resentment, bitterness, and regret, I'd be giving the devil control over my life. *James 4:7 (NIV)* declares, *"Submit yourselves, then, to God. Resist the devil, and he will flee from you."* I believed God wanted to heal and free me from what I allowed to control me, but in order to accept healing and freedom, I clearly needed to forgive.

Perhaps you can relate to my situation. Perhaps you are struggling to forgive another who's wronged you or perhaps there's a past regret you are struggling to let go. We do harm to ourselves by not surrendering to forgive others or what we have done to cause others pain.

I turned to a Lutheran minister, the husband to my friend and coworker, Rhonda, for help to forgive. He offered encouragement that I made the right decision to call off my engagement and commended my children for their wisdom and support. He directed me to a Christian counselor for guidance in whom he had confidence, and for good reason. The counselor was skilled with biblical knowledge and tools to help me find good in all circumstances, even those that are difficult. He called this technique "treasure hunting."

He helped me have better understanding of scripture. I especially liked *Genesis 50:20a (NIV), "You intended it to harm me, but God intended it for good to accomplish what is now being done."* I learned to practice *Psalms 84:11 (ASV), "No good thing will God withhold when you walk uprightly,"* and *Proverbs 21:21 (NIV), "Whoever pursues righteousness and love finds life, prosperity and honor."*

On the day of what would have been my wedding, I struggled. It fell on the weekend of Eric and Jenna's visit with their dad. It was a beautiful spring day with warmth, sunshine, and little wind. The grass turned to green and the birds were singing. It was the kind of day a bride wishes for on her wedding....a day for romance.

From the moment I stepped out of bed and on the patio and breathed in the beauty of the day, the words, "You really blew it," started in with me. The thought that I could be celebrating a joyous occasion on that beautiful day instead of spending it alone, led me to second guess my decision to call off my wedding.

I no more than pushed that thought aside and was reminded of the comment, "You're too particular…no one will ever measure up," that was spoken to me by someone several years past. My heart did not resonate with these thoughts or words; instead, it recognized that my spirit was under attack. To silence the chatter in my thoughts, I prayed for truth to drown out the lies. I called home to talk to my mom and dad. Both reassured me God wouldn't talk to me that way and that I made the right decision calling off my wedding. I busied myself after I got off the phone by painting Jenna's bedroom to keep from thinking about what a pretty day it was for a wedding.

After getting started, there was a knock at my door. It was my sister, Kate, and niece, Rylee, from out of town. They brought me a gift, a cross ornament with the words, "Believe in miracles" to remind me not to give up. God is so good. He cared enough to put it on my sister's heart to give a gift of encouragement and to spend the day with me, for He knew my spirit would be under attack. Kate arranged for her daughter, Rylee, and my sister, Loretta, to have lunch together and go to church.

> *How great is our Lord! His power is absolute!*
> *His understanding is beyond comprehension! (Psalm*
> *147:5 NLT)*

Before church, I visited with the priest in confession. I shared how I woke in the morning and struggled because the weather was just right for a wedding and chatter tried to convince me that I made a mistake and would never be satisfied. The priest assured me that I made the right decision to call off my wedding, for a Godly individual is a reflection of *Galatians 5:22–23 (NIV), "But the fruit of the Spirit is love, joy, peace, forbearance, kindness, goodness, faithfulness, gentleness and self-control."* He shared that God showed me His love through the beautiful weather that day and through my sisters' thoughtfulness. My heart found peace in the comfort and encouragement from the priest.

I asked, "How then will I ever trust again?"

His response was for me to do what I did in the past, to ask God to reveal truth where there is doubt. Again, I found peace in the priest's counsel.

> Know your worth. Never settle for less than
> you deserve. (Anonymous)

Not long after returning home from church, two of my brothers, Eddie and Alex, called to see how my day went; it was another way that God showed His love. Eddie and Alex assured me there are a few good men out there. I needed to hear that. I was thankful for the love of my family and for the reliability of God.

God turned what I thought would be a miserable day into a day of blessing! He confirmed for me that indeed I made the right decision by calling off my wedding.

> *You have looked deep into my heart, Lord,*
> *and you know all about me. You know when I am*
> *resting or when I am working, and from heaven*
> *you discover my thoughts. You notice everything I do*
> *and everywhere I go. Before I even speak a word, you*
> *know what I will say, and with your powerful arm*
> *you protect me from every side. I can't understand*
> *all of this! Such wonderful knowledge is far above*
> *me. (Psalm 139:1-6 CEV)*

Indeed, God is incredibly good and all powerful. Indeed also, it was time for me to move forward and grow from my experience. Through the power of the Holy Spirit and the help from the minister, the priest, my counselor, and loved ones, I was able to forgive, for God, not me, is the Judge and He is just.

It was necessary also that I do not pass judgement on my own self and not let regret of the mistake I made hinder my life and the lives of my children as well. If God and my children forgave me, then I also should forgive.

It was essential, I believed, to keep hope for a fulfilling marriage alive in my heart. The following week, I went to the dress shop where the wedding dress I planned to wear was stored. I made the final payment and took my dress home in hopes that one day I would wear it. I was confident that day would come!

> Yesterday is but today's memory, and tomorrow is today's dream. (Khalil Gibran)

Needing more of an income to provide for my family since school would soon be out for the summer, I prayed for a second job...a job that would fit into the schedule of my current job and not take my time from Eric and Jenna. Within days of applying for a position at a retail store in town for the early morning shift to unload stock, I received notice that there wasn't an opening for that particular position. That same day, I received notice of an unexpected bill. I refused to give in to worry, but instead put my faith in God to provide as He has done in the past.

Three days after receiving notification that the position I applied for wasn't available, I received a phone call from the store manager requesting an interview. It turned out a position became available and I was hired immediately following the interview. Praise God!

> *Let us hold tightly without wavering to the hope we affirm, for God can be trusted to keep his promises. (Hebrews 10:23 NLT)*

My second job didn't affect my lifestyle other than getting a few less hours of sleep three days out of the week. My position entailed unloading a truck filled with stock for the retail store several hours before dashing to the office at school. The adjustment wasn't enjoyable, but it did provide extra income for my family. The only adjustment for my children was Eric prepared breakfast for him and his sister and drove her and himself to school on the mornings I unloaded stock. I was blessed to have responsible children willing to do their part.

I enjoyed the remainder of the school year, feeling thankful that God is good and He is faithful. At the closing of that school year, I was offered a part-time summer job to work with special needs children through the school district that I worked for. The job worked nicely into my schedule to unload stock early in the morning before helping with the summer program at school until noon. Eric worked full-time with building construction for my nephew, Chad, and Jenna was allowed to join me at school to help with the children… God continued to provide, and I was grateful.

Just as it seemed I was walking on more solid ground, I encountered an experience I hadn't expected. Eric and I were headed to the grocery store for a few items. On our way to the entrance, we noticed my ex-fiancé's truck. What he was doing in town, I didn't know. Fear rose inside of me that I'd meet my used-to-be-fiancé face to face. "I can't go inside," I told Eric, "I don't want him to see me."

"We're going inside," Eric assured me and said to keep walking and concentrate on what we came to the store for.

My heart pounded as we made our way to the store. Once inside, my heart pounded more rapidly; there stood Robert. Fortunately, however, he didn't turn around to see me. Eric and I went about our business, gathered what we needed, and left the store without having to experience the awkwardness of seeing my ex face to face. As it turned out, God looked out for me even in that minor situation… my faith in Him grew a little bit stronger.

> Gratitude makes sense of our past, brings peace for today, and creates a vision for tomorrow. (Melody Beattie)

Points to Ponder

Perhaps, like me, you've allowed yourself to be mistreated and been in a situation so caught up in fear that you've lost focus on God's truth. Perhaps you dwell on what it cost to lose sight of His truth and you beat yourself for letting fear have control.

Let go of yesterday, my friend, and live for today. Stop beating yourself up, blaming others, and wallowing in pity. God forgives and wants you to forgive both yourself and others included. Just as we continue to love and to provide and care for our children when they make a mistake, our Lord does the same for us. He has great plans for you!

Do you struggle with knowing who you can trust?

Ask for truth and God will reveal it.

Have you been provided for time and time again?

Praise God and give Him glory!

Give thanks to the Lord, for he is good! His faithful love endures forever. (Psalm 136:1 NLT)

Prayer: Thank You, Jesus, that You are reliable, that You keep providing, and that You are faithful to forgive when I doubt, when I choose fear over truth, and when I do wrong. Forgive me please, for the times I struggle to forgive others or even myself. Thank You for teaching me truth and for bringing good out of a bad situation. Open my heart to the lessons You want to teach me and use the hurt I have been caused to grow me into the person You want me to be. Help me, Jesus, to recognize when my spirit is under attack and please replace lies that I believe with Your truth. Help me to learn from my failures and to forgive not only those who wrong me, but myself for the choices I make that please the devil instead of You. Thank You, Father, for the healing that comes through forgiveness. Thank You for sending me a friend when I need one and for showing Your love for me in the beauty of each new day. I pray this in Your precious name, Jesus. Amen.

Chapter 8

LEARN

Depend on the LORD; trust him, and he will take care of you.

—Psalm 37:5 (NCV)

It was nice to have the summer off like I had been used to in the past. Aside from helping with summer school for a month and unloading the truck early in the morning, I was free to spend more time with my parents and my children. I had time to enjoy hobbies like gardening, walking, and bicycling and to attend Jenna's softball games. I even went out on a few dates, but didn't, however, connect with anyone.

Daydreaming one day about true love and wondering when it would be mine with a companion, the song, "By Your Side," by Tenth Avenue North came on the radio. The lyrics shifted my thoughts, for they asked the question why I was still searching as if God wasn't enough. I sensed that God was speaking to my heart to simply enjoy what He gave at the time and to stop searching for something I wasn't yet ready for.

Only days later, I was driving in the car with Jenna and sharing my hopes about one day having a fulfilling marriage. I no more than started sharing and the same song played again on the radio.

"Strange," I said, "this song played just the other day when I was thinking about a fulfilling marriage."

Jenna said, "I think God's telling you to be patient and let Him bring it in His time."

I knew in my heart that's what God was telling me. I believed He used Jenna to confirm that He spoke a message to my heart through a song.

> *For ye have need of patience, that, after ye have*
> *done the will of God, ye might receive the promise.*
> *(Hebrews 10:36 KJV)*

Perhaps you're waiting for a dream to come to pass and the Holy Spirit is prompting you as well to be patient and enjoy the blessings God has given you until the time is right.

Not long after realizing that God used a song to speak a message to me, I was driving to work early in the morning and was moved by another song, "Before the Morning," by Josh Wilson. The words to this song ask if you wonder why you have to feel the things that hurt you. The artist expresses that there may be things we can't see, but these things happen to bring better endings and that someday we will understand. The lyrics inspired me to have hope for my future. Before going inside to work, I took a moment to thank God for speaking encouragement to my heart.

> A life watered by tears of tragedy and suffer-
> ing often becomes the most fertile soil for spiri-
> tual growth. (Unknown)

Starting that moment, I prayed that God would prepare my true love and me for each other, that God would watch over us and grow us into who He wants us to be.

> *Cast your cares on the LORD and he will sus-*
> *tain you; he will never let the righteous be shaken.*
> *(Psalm 55:22 NIV)*

141

Because God proved His faithfulness in the past, I set my mind on trusting Him to provide and to answer my prayers. I started seeing myself as blessed with the life I wanted instead of feeling sorry for myself and questioning whether my dreams would ever come true.

> If you fell down yesterday, stand up today.
> (H. G. Wells)

Eric turned sixteen years old that summer and Jenna eleven years old. We were able to do some fishing and camping in our tent with friends. We rode the family bicycle, go carts, and bumper boats at the campground as well. Life was good! I was thankful for my relationship with my children and for the friends we had.

Eric and Jenna were thoughtful. They put a video together with the help of their dad that included photos of memories we've shared, along with one of my favorite songs, "What Faith Can Do," by Kutless playing in the background. In this song the artist encourages me not to give up because of dreams that can move mountains, because of hope that doesn't end even when times are tough, because of miracles that happen, and because of silent prayers that get answered all because of faith.

There were things I may not have had, but what I had was more valuable than what I lacked. God blessed me well.

When school started up, Eric entered his sophomore year in high school and Jenna started fifth grade. Our house was rarely empty as was the table when it came time for supper. Often Eric's buddy, Connor, and my daughter's friends visited and joined us for meals. They even joined us on occasion when we drove back to our hometown for Eric and Jenna to visit their dad Wednesdays after school.

It felt good to be back at school. I sure enjoyed my job as the secretary. Although I was appreciative of my second job, I can't say I enjoyed it as much. Having to wake early to work two jobs and being responsible for what needed tending to at home wasn't the schedule I wanted to keep for long, but a schedule I knew I had to have for the time being.

After keeping up with my busy schedule for several months, I ran into my cousin, John, who shared that his friend, Bill, the owner of a hunting and wedding lodge, whom I met while operating the hunting lodge back home, inquired about me. As it turned out, Bill needed help with his lodge and wondered if I was available.

I contacted Bill to let him know I was in the area and possibly available to help him. To my surprise, he offered for me to manage his lodge a few miles out of town in the country. I thought back to the satisfaction I got from helping operate the two lodges back home. I saw the offer as an opportunity for financial stability. God is good!

I kept my full-time job at school, but gave up my early morning job unloading the truck at the retail store in exchange to manage the wedding aspect of the lodge and to help when available during the hunting season.

Thankful for my new job, I got right to scrubbing walls and washing out cabinets at the lodge with the help of my children and a couple of their friends. When the school year ended, they helped me prepare for the first wedding of the season. While I hung décor, washed the bedding, and weeded the flower beds, Eric and his friend, Connor, cut the grass, strung the lights, and disposed of trash. Jenna washed dishes and explored the grounds with her friend, Caressa. When the work was completed, we sat back and admired the ambiance of the lodge and its courtyard. What a privilege it was to care for this beautiful place in the country and have the help of my children and friends.

At that time, Eric had just started dating his friend, Lauren, who fit nicely into our family. It didn't take long for her to be a part of all of our lives and for me to love her as my own. I especially enjoyed the smile she put on my son's face. I enjoyed cooking and baking with her and Eric, who liked being in charge in the kitchen. I admired how Eric cared for Lauren, made her a priority, and still welcomed my company. I recall the time when Eric had his wisdom teeth removed. He was unable to drive due to pain medication, so he and Jenna and I picked Lauren up from her house to watch a movie with us at our house. After the movie, we giggled and piled back into the car to take Lauren back to her house. That was one of many fond memories I have of getting to be a part of the moments Eric and Lauren spent together.

Between running Jenna back and forth that summer to friends and her softball practices and games, driving back home to visit my parents and my children's dad, managing the lodge, and keeping up with chores at home, it was busy, however enjoyable. I took pride in managing the lodge and its events and enjoyed Eric and Jenna's help. Busy as it was, there was still time for camping and fishing with Eric, Lauren, and Jenna as well as time for taking in a few car races that Eric introduced me to.

Before that summer came to a close, Eric made the suggestion that we take a vacation, something I hadn't done with my children due to our budget. He said we didn't have to go far or make it a fancy trip, but just go somewhere to relax a few days and take in a new experience. So Eric, Lauren, Jenna, and I headed to a nearby town a few hours away for a little getaway. We spent part of our trip at a water park with a large water slide that I was certain I wouldn't ride. That was until Eric and Jenna convinced me to give it just one try. I did, and it was fun! We enjoyed several other attractions, one of which was a butterfly museum where the butterflies were attracted to Eric. There I saw a stepping stone with the words inscribed, "Chase the butterfly all over the field and you may never catch it, but sit quietly on the grass and it will come to you and sit upon your shoulders," that encouraged me to sit quietly and wait for the desires of my heart.

I was glad we took the trip and thankful for the good time we had and for the memories we made.

Then a suddenly happened! In August, while the county fair was taking place in our community, my good and dear friend, Rebecca, from school called me up to invite me to come to the fairgrounds where she had a booth set up. She met a man from a nearby town whom she was certain was the man I had been praying for.

It had been a long day for me at the lodge, and truthfully, I was hesitant about meeting a man that my friend just met. I thanked Rebecca for thinking of me, but explained that I was going to pass because I was tired from the busy day.

I prepared supper for my family and gave little thought to this man Rebecca believed was "the one" for me. Jenna assured me if I was meant to meet him, our paths would cross. I agreed…she had sensible thinking.

The following evening Jenna asked if we could go back to the fair one more time. Having already been there a couple of nights during the week, I wasn't keen on going back, but I gave in since the fair comes but once a year.

At the fair, I visited with my friend who called me on the phone the previous evening. It just so happened that while we were visiting, the man she told me about came by. Rebecca introduced us to each other and we talked for the next hour or so. I learned he lived in a community not too far from the community where I lived and had two daughters close in age to my children.

I couldn't help but admire the sincerity in the man I just met, the tenderness in his eyes, and gentleness in his smile. Ryan appeared to be genuine…perhaps my friend was right about this man being the one. Ryan appeared to have a lot of characteristics that I had been looking for in a companion.

Before saying goodbye, Ryan asked if he could call me. I whole-heartedly said, "Yes." Jenna, who apparently was observing while she walked around with her friend, Ava, gave permission as well for him to call me. I called Eric on our way home to share what happened.

My heart felt a bit giddy, I must admit, as I thought about the possibility of a future with Ryan. He was more than I was expecting when Rebecca described him. I was eager to learn more about him in which I was given the opportunity the following evening when he called. We both had a lot to share as well as to ask. Ryan gave me the impression that he was genuinely interested in wanting to know more about me and that what he shared was said in truth. At the end of our conversation, he asked if he could call again.

Eric teased when I got off the phone that it must have been some phone call to put a smile that big on my face. He requested to meet Ryan before the relationship went any farther which was only right. In fact, I was honored that he made the request. It showed me that he cared. I admired the way Eric looked out for his sister and me, and for his girlfriend. It was a role he took on without being asked. What a fine young man!

School started up that following Monday. I arrived at the office with a twinkle in my eye as did Rebecca. She proudly announced to other staff members that she was responsible for being matchmaker over the weekend. She was a kind-hearted, fun-loving person who enjoyed making others happy.

Meeting someone I was interested in wasn't the only reason I had a twinkle in my eye. Jenna, now twelve years old and in the sixth grade, moved from the elementary school level to the middle school level where I got to see her at the change of every class. I liked that I worked within the school district where I got to be a part of Eric and Jenna's day at school every day. Jenna continued with sports and dance, so evenings continued to be busy for us.

Eric, now seventeen, entered his junior year in high school. He continued working a couple of hours after school with his cousin, Chad, who owned a construction company.

Two weeks after school was back in session, Ryan came to see me. He was in town for the weekend visiting his parents. He and my son met and carried on a pleasant conversation before we went out for an evening walk. They both appeared comfortable and at ease with each other. Actually, Eric gave me the thumbs up and said he liked Ryan. It was important that I had the approval of both my son and my daughter.

I enjoyed walking with Ryan and discovering more about his experiences and hopes for the future. I enjoyed, too, the hint of fall that approached the late evening air. We thanked each other for the nice time we had and parted for the night.

The next morning, Eric, Jenna, and I headed out of town to pick up supplies for Eric's truck. Our conversation during the drive was lighthearted and positive as we reminisced and shared hopes for our future. On our way, we drove through the town where Ryan lived. I took in the beautiful scenery and visualized living back in the country in a home with my family with a quiet space for me to write.

I let my mind drift to dream about all that I wanted. I wondered if Ryan was the one God sent for me to love.

I fixed supper for my family when we arrived home and accepted the offer for another walk with Ryan. This time he took my hand in his as we stepped off the patio to start our walk. The air was crisp that evening with more of a chill than the evening before, giving Ryan opportunity to wrap his arms around my waist at the end of our walk to warm me. His touch was gentle. It offered a sense of security. We said, "Goodnight" and parted with a gentle kiss on the lips.

When I arrived back in the house, Eric and his girlfriend, Lauren, teased that I looked like a teenager in love. I felt like one. I liked Ryan and admired his quiet, gentle, and sensitive spirit. I felt safe in his presence.

In the morning, after church, Eric, Lauren, Jenna, and I drove a couple of hours to the state fair where my sister, Kate, her husband, and their daughter, Rylee, lived. We enjoyed taking in the fair together and visiting with my sister and her family. While there, a text message came through from Ryan. Eric, Lauren, and Jenna all gathered to see the message as though they were all a part of the relationship with Ryan. They were in a sense, and I was happy they took an interest.

Ryan's message was simple...just telling me he was thinking of me. I felt pretty light on my feet. I believed what started with Ryan was a good thing. I looked forward to my parents meeting him.

> *He put a new song in my mouth, a song of praise to our God. (Psalm 40:3 ESV)*

POINTS TO PONDER

Are you looking forward for a dream to come to pass and enjoying what you have while you wait or are you growing impatient as though God is not enough?

Satan wants to keep you stuck as a prisoner of doubt, fear, worry, and regret. He reminds you of your mistakes, steals your hope, and tries to convince you that you will never amount to anything.

God, on the other hand, wants to give you hope, my friend, lift your spirits, and put a new song in your heart.

But I trust in your unfailing love. I will rejoice
because you have rescued me. (Psalm 13:5 NLT)

Prayer: Dear and gracious Lord, thank You for being so good to me and for blessing me with opportunity to be a part of my loved ones' joys. Forgive me, please, for the times I have been impatient while You have been working behind the scenes to bring blessings into my life. Help me to enjoy what I have at the present time and to keep hope in Your promises. Help me to learn the lessons You want me to learn from past mistakes, to forgive in all circumstances, and to open my heart to trust again. Help me to see me the way You see me and to have faith that You can move mountains. I pray this in Your precious name. Amen.

Chapter 9

GOD KNOWS

LORD Almighty, blessed is the one who trusts in you.

—Psalm 84:12 (NIV)

From that weekend on, Ryan called every evening to ask how my day went and to say goodnight. He sent emails throughout the day, visited on the weekends, and sent me a rose at work and a card in the mail on the twenty-first of every month in honor of when we met. I felt happy, cared for, and special in Ryan's eyes.

My parents, siblings, nieces, and nephews got to meet Ryan a couple of months into our relationship at my mom and dad's fifty-eighth wedding anniversary. Friends, family, and coworkers were happy for me and believed I found my true love, as did my children and me.

I was drawn to Ryan's sensitive and soft-spoken spirit. The more I got to know him, the more I noticed our personalities seemed alike. There was a quiet, peaceful nature to both of us. We both were sentimental, fun-loving, and caring. We appreciated family, the tranquility and awe of nature, and what giving and laughter do for the soul. Our dreams were similar as far as desiring well-being for the mind, body, and spirit. We shared the passion of wanting to share with others our gifts and knowledge of taking care of oneself and loved ones.

My heart felt peace with Ryan. I was in love with him. I believed his heart to be trustworthy.

I enjoyed spending time with his parents, both very kind-hearted and dear, as well as with his family. I was sure my heart found a home with Ryan. I prayed for him and his family to be blessed with God's goodness.

I prayed for happiness for Brad too. I wished him a love so true.

Feeling in love made me look forward to Christmas. I had the feeling that I would be proposed to even though it had only been four months that I had been dating Ryan. He and I attended the Christmas Eve service at church with my children and one of his daughters, opened presents at my house, and spent the rest of the evening with his family and my children and Lauren at his parents' house. I wasn't proposed to like I expected, but I wasn't disappointed because I was confident and happy in our relationship and certain the time would come. We spent Christmas Day with my family at my mom and dad's house.

After returning to my house from spending Christmas Day with my family, there was one more present for me to open. My heart raced with anticipation that it might be an engagement ring. It wasn't, but I was still happy. The present was actually something I pointed out when we were together, which made me appreciative that Ryan was mindful of what I liked. He then invited me to sit next to him under the Christmas tree with the lights aglow to dream about tomorrow and take in one last moment for a memory of that Christmas Day.

Fumbling with the little house with twenty-five doors that sat under my tree which previously had a treat behind each door, Ryan suggested that we check all of the doors to make sure the treats had all been found and taken out. I laughed and playfully helped him check each of the doors, one by one. And there it was—an engagement ring, behind door number twenty-five! My heart skipped! I felt honored to say, "Yes" to Ryan when he proposed to me. He slipped the ring on my finger.

Eric and Jenna were happy for me as were family and friends. My mom and dad couldn't have been more pleased as they were quite fond of Ryan. Going back to work after the Christmas break and getting to share my exciting news with friends and coworkers was an exciting time.

It was Ryan's plan to sell his home and commute back and forth to work. He seemed eager to make plans, so we contacted the priest where my children and I attended church and got started with marriage preparation.

We chose the fall season for our wedding and our children as our attendants, along with Ryan's brother, Collin, and my sister, Kate. We both took part in planning for our wedding day and put careful thought into picking the scripture and songs for our ceremony. I truly looked forward to my life with Ryan who I connected with so well. To family and friends, we were the perfect match.

Therefore my heart is glad, and my whole being rejoices; my flesh also dwells secure. (Psalm 16:9 ESV)

It was a proud moment for me to watch my son get fitted for his tux for his high school junior prom that he attended with Lauren that spring, and an even prouder moment when he got fitted for my wedding in which he and his sister would be escorting me down the aisle. I was honored to have Eric, Lauren, and Jenna all with me the day I was fitted for my wedding gown, the one previously chosen several years ago that I stored in hopes to be used. It felt good to have all of us together at that special moment. I treasured the closeness and the love between us.

With summer coming to an end and my wedding only a month away, another school year began. Eric, eighteen years old, was already a senior and Jenna, thirteen years old, already a teenager, went into the seventh grade.

As the day approached closer to my wedding, I thought more and more of the changes that lie ahead. Having a husband after being on my own for eight years was going to take some adjusting as was having to let go of my son for college after sheltering him for nineteen years. It was necessary to keep a positive frame of mind and in line with the Holy Spirit, for I was in no way ready to let go of Eric. The thought of gaining a husband, however, helped with the idea of having to let go of him.

> *For if they fall, the one will lift up his fellow:*
> *but woe to him that is alone when he falleth; for he*
> *hath not another to help him up. (Ecclesiastics 4:10*
> *KJV)*

The weekend of my wedding arrived. Ryan was in town a couple of days early to help with the finishing touches and to make sure his tux fit. I smiled as I watched him and Eric pose in their tuxes and laugh because Eric's tux was a couple of sizes off. It put a smile on my heart, too, to watch Jenna adjust the tie on Ryan's shirt. I enjoyed that kind of fun-loving, peaceful atmosphere that I had been used to with my children. I was confident it would remain after being married.

After making adjustments on Eric's tux, finalizing last-minute wedding preparations, and running through the rehearsal a couple of times, we were all set and I was at peace. That was until I noticed a distant feeling from Ryan during and after the rehearsal supper.

It had been a busy and long day for both Ryan and me, but it was unlike either of us to discount the other. I understood pre-wedding jitters, but what I sensed seemed more than just a slight nervousness. Ryan appeared sad. I gave him the benefit of doubt, though, when he expressed what a long day it had been. He kissed me goodnight and took off for his mom and dad's house where he and his daughters spent the night.

Still unsure the morning of my wedding about Ryan's distant behavior the evening before, I expressed concern to Jenna on the way to the hair salon for our appointment. Jenna reassured me that she's sure it's normal to feel nervous the day of or the day before the wedding. I expressed the same concern to Eric when I arrived home before he drove me to the church. I sat on the foot of his bed as I shared while he gathered his clothes. Eric knew how important it was that I marry the man God intended. He could tell I was concerned.

He paused from getting ready for the day, extended a hug as he so often did, and reassured me that Ryan was a good man and we were doing the right thing.

My heart calmed and was more at peace after being reassured by both my son and daughter. I wasn't yet sure what it was that made Ryan appear to be sad the night before.

Time was running out. Lauren, my personal attendant, was waiting. She called Eric to tell him to hurry with me. I couldn't help but smile when Eric chuckled, "Don't worry. She's with me." Feeling blessed, I felt like the happiest mom in the world. I was honored to have my son drive me to the church on my wedding day and thankful that both my children were supportive of me remarrying.

Upon arriving to the church and seeing Ryan after I was in my gown, my heart lightened. He was smiling, back to himself, and stunning in his tuxedo. The safe and secure feeling I was used to in our relationship settled back into my heart... I was relieved.

All set for the ceremony, Jenna looked beautiful with her hair done up and her dress that fit just right, Eric was handsome in his black tuxedo with Lauren, the attractive young woman that stole his heart, next to his side, and my parents were looking proud and so happy for me.

Then there was me, the bride. Feeling more beautiful than ever, I took one last look in the mirror and made my way to the entrance of the church where Eric and Jenna waited to escort me down the aisle to lead me to the man they trusted would give his love and care with all his heart.

Moments later, I was joined in marriage with Ryan and greeted by guests from both sides of our family. We then headed to the wedding lodge that I was still managing, to celebrate with a meal and dance for all our guests.

After having the first dance with Ryan, I danced a special dance with both Eric and Jenna and my parents to the song, "Because You Loved Me," by Celine Dion. My heart resonates with the lyrics because the artist expresses sincere gratitude toward someone special who stood by her, helped her see truth, and brought joy to her life just like my family did for me. Like Celine expresses in her song, my parents and children saw me through my struggles, believed in me, and supported me. They were my eyes when I couldn't see and saw the best in me no matter my circumstance. I was blessed by their inspiration and a better person because they loved me just like Celine's song expresses... I will forever be grateful because of the beautiful love of my family.

Perhaps you too have been blessed with gifts so precious that you also feel thankful.

After an enjoyable celebration with friends and family, we settled in for the night at the lodge for an early rise to clean in the morning with help from our family.

> Feeling grateful or appreciative of someone
> or something in your life actually attracts more
> of the things that you appreciate and value into
> your life. (Northrup Christiane)

POINTS TO PONDER

What precious and priceless gifts has God blessed you with?

Do you find yourself thanking Him frequently for the beautiful blessings He has given, or do you sometimes forget and take for granted the good that you have?

Be mindful at all times, my friend, for thanking our Lord for the good He has done for you.

> *I will extol the LORD at all times; his praise*
> *will always be on my lips. (Psalm 34:1 NIV)*

Prayer: Good and dear Jesus, thank You for the many gifts You have given me. Forgive me for the times I may have forgotten to thank You. Thank You for knowing what is best and for not holding back on the good that You give. Help me never to doubt the promises You make or take for granted, the love You have for me, and the gifts You give. Let praise for You forever be on my lips. In Your precious name, I pray. Amen.

Chapter 10

TRUST

Fear not, for I am with you; be not dismayed, for I am your God. I will strengthen you, yes, I will help you, I will uphold you with My righteous right hand.

—Isaiah 41:10 (NKJV)

At the morning's rise, Ryan was distant once more. He appeared sad, very sad, but I didn't know why. Wishing I'd have heard, "Good morning my love," instead of, "I couldn't sleep," I got dressed and remained silent for fear of what I'd hear…that perhaps he regretted getting married.

When clean-up from our reception and dance was complete, I got inside the car with Ryan and headed for the home we planned for "ours" instead of "mine." The silence continued. Something seemed terribly wrong. Neither of us liked confrontation, but one of us was going to have to speak. Either I was going to have to ask what was going on or Ryan was going to have to share.

Ryan spoke. He confessed that he couldn't keep the promise he made to me at the altar the day before on our wedding. He shared that he needed time before he could commit to being the husband I was expecting.

My heart sank because of what I had just heard. I didn't understand. Ryan and I couldn't wait for the time to come to be together and to show an example of true love and commitment to our children. I didn't know what had gone wrong. What we had seemed real. *Where did it go?*

Ryan helped me carry what was left of food and decorations from the wedding inside when we arrived at my house and then said goodbye. I felt numb. I stood confused and speechless as I watched him drive off to go back to his home that hadn't yet sold. I felt betrayed, rejected, lied to, misled, and let down. My dream for "happily ever after" with Ryan and our children felt shattered.

I struggled for the words when my children asked what was going on. No one would have expected Ryan to turn from his promise. He was nothing but loving and seemingly committed while we dated. We had the kind of relationship others desired.

I didn't know how I'd face coworkers come Monday morning or cover the hurt my heart was feeling. What was I to say; they witnessed nothing but the look of bliss in my eyes and a glowing happiness in the past year that I dated the man I truly believed loved me. I didn't want anyone to hear of my struggle, know that I was hurting, or that my husband may have been unsure. I didn't want to answer to "congratulations" or comments about my wedding.

Besides my son and daughter, the only other who knew what had happened was my good friend, Rebecca, who introduced Ryan and I to each other the previous year. She dropped by with a present all excited to visit us the evening after our wedding, but instead found Ryan not there and me in tears.

I didn't want to go to work the next day. I wanted to be alone to cry and figure out what had gone wrong so it could be fixed. As it turned out, Jenna got ill during the night which kept me from going to work come Monday morning. I took that time to sort through what had happened, hoping to get through to Ryan.

I heard from him that day. He shared that he woke to the song, "No Doubt About It," by Neil McCoy, playing in his head the morning of our wedding at 5:30 AM. He expressed that I was the one he was dreaming of and believed, without a doubt, that we were meant to be together just like the lyrics express in the song. What was strange, he said, was that he hadn't heard that song in a long time. He shared that he honestly believed in his heart that he married the right person.

I wanted to believe Ryan. I believed he really did love me, that he meant well, and that he never meant to cause any hurt. I believed, too, that he was a good person. What I questioned was whether his heart had been healed from his first marriage that had failed. After giving what had happened some thought, I was certain it wasn't. I understood when I met Ryan, he had gone through quite an ordeal, but I believed him when he said he was ready to move on. I believed, too, that I could help heal with my love any part of Ryan that may still have been hurting.

After taking Monday off, both Jenna and I went back to school the following day. From the moment I arrived at work, coworkers and friends commented on my wedding throughout the day with congratulations and compliments of how beautiful the wedding was and how beautiful we all looked. I thanked them politely and pretended to be happy. I couldn't wait for the workday to end so I could be alone to cry and figure out where to go from there.

I got angry at Ryan for putting our marriage in the position it was in. It appeared to me that he withheld truth until after our wedding. I felt hurt from feeling rejected and bitter for feeling neglected. All I could think was, *How could this be happening?*

Luckily, my coworkers fell for my cover up. At least I thought they did. The ones I was closest to suspected something wasn't right. I shared briefly that Ryan had some things to take care of before moving in, but kept quiet for the most part so not to bring my personal life into the workplace. When I was at home, however, it was a different story. I cried and did my share of complaining. Eric and Jenna listened, but didn't know what to say. None of us saw coming what had happened.

Perhaps you're experiencing a similar situation. Perhaps you're lost for answers as far as fixing a situation you don't understand.

I didn't want my parents to know what had happened. Like me, they too longed for love to be mine. I knew they'd be concerned and

157

hurt to hear of my circumstance; I didn't want them to worry and be sad. I was sure Ryan would move in with me within the next couple of weeks and that we'd be able to work through our circumstance.

Like me, you may be covering truth as well to protect the ones you love. It's not wrong to want to protect our loved ones, but keeping truth hidden isn't necessarily the answer or even possible in all situations.

There wasn't a way that I could keep from telling my parents that Ryan wasn't with me. During a visit from them at my house, I shared what had happened. They hurt of course, like a parent would, but I reassured them that I was okay and all would be well.

I tried getting through to Ryan over the phone that we shouldn't be apart. No words of encouragement or advice could convince him to pack his belongings though and move in together. I could tell from the tone of his voice that he felt bad because of our circumstance. He may have needed more healing than I thought.

Relieved that the weekend finally arrived so I could have a break from comments and questions from coworkers about my wedding and marriage, I longed for quiet time with God. With Him I didn't have to pretend.

Exhausted from carrying the burden of trying to reason with my husband the past week, I asked at the end of the working day on Friday on my way out the door, "Why, God, have I been rejected again?"

"This too will make you stronger" is the response that rang in my spirit.

I didn't like what I heard. I didn't want to go through the hurt of another rejection. I pounded my fists on the steering wheel of my car the moment I got inside and cried, "Haven't You given me enough already to make me strong?"

It seemed God responded loud and clear to my cry with a song the very moment I turned the ignition to start the car. "Stronger," by Mandisa, came on the radio. Her song hit home with me. She sang about someone dwelling on their life not going right and wondering if things will ever get better. She encouraged to fall into the arms of Jesus and not to hang their head, but to hang on because the circumstance is going to end, God is there, He will be faithful, and the experience is going to make them stronger.

Still sitting in my car in the parking lot at school, I bowed my head on the steering wheel. "Why?" I pleaded, "Why, God, do I need to be stronger?"

Perhaps you too are desperate for an answer because your heart is confused and hurting.

It seemed God promptly responded quickly and clearly again with yet another song. "Blessings," by Laura Story, immediately followed the previous song. My heart was reminded that God brings blessings out of our trials after hearing the song present the questions, what if blessings come through raindrops, healing comes through tears, and if our trials in life are our mercies in disguise? I was touched in such a way by God's response that all I could say was, "Thank you, God… I'm sorry."

I shifted my car into gear and headed for home. I believed with all my heart God would carry me through the storm and bless me according to His will. Blessings weren't going to come, however, by complaining, whining, and pitying myself like I had been doing that week and that day. I needed to rise, take up my bed, and walk like the lame man by the pool of Bethesda whom God healed. *"When Jesus saw him lying there, and knew that he already had been in that condition a long time, He said to him, 'Do you want to be made well?' The sick man answered Him, 'Sir, I have no man to put me into the pool when the water is stirred up; but while I am coming, another steps down before me.' Jesus said to him, 'Rise, take up your bed and walk.' And immediately the man was made well, took up his bed, and walked"* (John 5:6–9 NKJV).

After arriving home from work, Eric asked for me to go with him to the sport and bait shop. While on our way, I shared the experience I had in the school parking lot. Eric agreed to stay encouraged that God would keep His promise and bring good out of my struggle and grow me stronger. He shared also that he believed the song was a sign from God that Ryan was a good man and meant well. I could always count on my children to offer support and encouragement. I didn't take that blessing from God for granted.

Eric no more than spoke words of encouragement when the song Ryan had playing in his mind the morning of our wedding, "No Doubt About It," started playing in my son's truck.

"Is this a CD playing?" I asked Eric.

"No," he said, "it's the radio."

I hadn't heard that song in years. I believed it was so that Ryan indeed was meant to be in my life and that because of my circumstance, I would be blessed.

After sharing with Ryan that the song that ran through his thoughts the morning of our wedding played on the radio, he reassured me that we'd get through the struggle we were facing and that he knew what he needed to do. I was hopeful and believed Ryan that he would take the step needed to commit to our marriage. I was willing to be patient and offer support to him.

Weeks passed with no change. I felt like a failure, like I did something wrong and let Ryan down, though I didn't know where. We went from an enjoyable courtship to a broken marriage overnight without any explanation, yet Ryan expressed a desire to stay married. The fear of leaving behind what he wasn't ready to let go of, however, perhaps had such a hold over Ryan that he felt safer staying where he was.

Wanting to work through our circumstance, I suggested to Ryan that we visit with the pastor I visited with awhile back, or with a priest, my counselor, or a counselor of his choice. I even suggested for Ryan to go on his own if he preferred. Ryan agreed to visit with the pastor and invited me to join him. The pastor discussed the roles and responsibilities of a husband and a wife. The more he encouraged Ryan to commit to our marriage, however, the more distant Ryan appeared. I was used to him leaving love notes behind when he visited while we dated and talking nonstop about dreams for our future. Once married though, conversation grew scarce and notes were nowhere to be found. I missed the man I fell in love with. I struggled with the request he made to remain apart except for the weekends. Ryan's request left me to feel as though I was a burden to him.

Not wanting to stand in the way of something dear to Ryan that he seemingly wasn't ready to let go of, I stepped aside and offered him the time he needed over the Christmas holiday to sort through whatever it was he struggled to let go of. Spending the holiday without the man who proposed to me the year before under the Christmas tree wasn't what I expected the following year, but I wasn't going to let my situation bring my spirits down. I trusted God would use the situation for good. It wasn't necessary to know how, but encouraging that in time it indeed would unfold.

> *Do not let your hearts be troubled. You believe*
> *in God; believe also in me. (John 14:1 NIV)*

I enjoyed attending the Christmas service with Eric, Lauren, and Jenna, and gathering with my family back home for a meal. We spent the later part of the day at Eric and Jenna's dad's house and exchanged presents with him. He was aware of the circumstance between Ryan and me and offered to listen and share what he learned from our circumstance in our marriage. Brad learned how important it is to listen to your partner's needs and to make them a priority. He and I both learned from our situation. We grew stronger, wiser, and better because of it. I actually felt closer to him than I had ever felt. I appreciated his kindness.

I used the Christmas break from work to reflect on the past three months of my marriage. I prayed to get through yet another storm and for strength from our Lord to stand tall for the sake of my children. I did not want them to know how badly I was hurting or to see me fall apart.

> *I know what it is to be in need, and I know*
> *what it is to have plenty. I have learned the secret of*
> *being content in any and every situation, whether*
> *well fed or hungry, whether living in plenty or in*
> *want. I can do all this through him who gives me*
> *strength. (Philippians 4:12–13 NIV)*

I enjoyed this time with my children and Lauren over the break since we were all off from school. We baked and decorated sugar cookies, cuddled on the couch for a movie, and took in a hockey game too. I sure appreciated what time my children still enjoyed spending with me and how nicely Lauren blended in our family.

Christmas break ended and school started back up for all of us. While my wait continued for Ryan to make a move, I appreciated the blessings present in my life and found strength in our Lord to keep hope that my marriage would take a turn for the better.

After months of being separated from Ryan, he came to see me. While embracing in one another's arms after all that time, Ryan expressed that he was ready to let go of the past, to accept help, to trust God, and to make necessary changes to live as husband and wife. Praise God for his change of heart! I looked forward to the change that it appeared to me Ryan desired.

> *Praise the* LORD. *Give thanks to the LORD, for he is good; his love endures forever. (Psalm 106:1 NIV)*

POINTS TO PONDER

Perhaps you're in a place of suffering, feeling rejected, or feeling disappointed. Perhaps, like me, you're trying to hide your pain. If so, where are you turning to for comfort, hope, security, and strength in your time of suffering?

Perhaps you're praying for the suffering to be removed. Or perhaps you don't like the response the Lord provided.

Dear one, our Lord knows your pain and will provide the strength you need to get through the storm and come out stronger. Believe that when God starts something in your life, He will be faithful to complete it and to keep His promises. He can turn your hurts into blessings. Bring your hurt to the Lord, friend. With Him you don't have to pretend.

> *And we know that in all things God works*
> *for the good of those who love him, who have been*
> *called according to his purpose. (Romans 8:28 NIV)*

Prayer: Heavenly Father, thank You that I can trust You to keep Your promises. I'm sorry for the times I don't like the response I get from You. Help me to turn to You in my times of disappointment, times of suffering, or times when I don't know what to do. Help me to accept Your response even when I don't understand. Please give me the strength, Jesus, and the grace to pick up my mat, to put my trust in You, and to walk in the confidence of knowing I will be made well, stronger, and blessed indeed. I pray this in Your holy name, Lord Jesus. Amen.

Chapter 11

GOD GIVES

For the LORD God is a sun and shield: the LORD will give grace and glory: no good thing will he withhold from them that walk uprightly.

—Psalm 84:11 (KJV)

I prayed that Ryan and I would grow deeper in our love for the Lord and for one another. We continued counseling with the pastor who we met with awhile back. The pastor was compassionate about our circumstance, but firm with instruction to obey the Lord in all ways. We also met with the priest who had instructed us with marriage preparation while we were still dating. He too was firm in teaching obedience of our Lord. Both the pastor and the priest advised Ryan and me to seek marriage counseling as well. We took their advice and started counseling with the counselor I had been seeing.

Was it all too overwhelming for Ryan? I didn't know. But I sensed he felt pressured from all directions which gave me concern that he may lack desire to follow through with necessary changes. One side of me felt led to hold back from expressing my needs as a wife. Expressing my needs seemed only to make Ryan shut down. The other side of me felt led to stand firm, set boundaries, and not settle.

What was I to do? Holding back from expressing my needs seemed to enable Ryan to stay stuck and not make a change. Love and relationships can't grow if one or both of the partners suppresses their thoughts and feelings. Yet standing firm in my belief for Ryan to pick up his mat as well and walk appeared too aggressive for him. Neither of the two seemed effective.

I learned already that forcing others only pushes them away. I couldn't risk pushing Ryan any farther than he already was or I may have lost him for sure. Yet I wasn't willing to be neglected and mistreated like I felt I was after my wedding day.

I made a decision to support Ryan by encouraging him as best I could in a positive manner. It wasn't easy staying committed to being positive when it appeared that my husband was indecisive.

One of the suggestions the pastor made during counseling was for Ryan to commit to commuting back and forth from work to my house during the weekdays that he didn't have his daughter who lived with him part-time. Ryan agreed and arrived promptly to my house for supper an hour after his workday was completed. There seemed to be an obvious unease, however, that I already sensed the first evening. I sensed Ryan didn't enjoy the drive to my house after a long day at work, which led to me accepting guilt. I didn't feel good about him having to do something he didn't seem to enjoy.

Only days into giving the pastor's idea a try, I shared with him and Ryan that I was uncomfortable asking Ryan to do something if it truly wasn't in his heart to do. I wanted Ryan to be with me because he wanted to, rather than feeling pressured like he may have felt. The pastor understood my feelings. Ryan agreed that the visits were uncomfortable; he went back to visiting me on the weekends. It was disheartening to see him arrive at my doorstep with his overnight bag late Friday evening after a visit with his parents and then leave to go back to what he was used to Sunday afternoon. After experiencing the tension from Ryan's visits during the week, however, weekend visits felt less uncomfortable than forcing him to do what it appeared he didn't want to do. I vowed to give it my best to give him the time he needed to be the man I believed God wanted him to be.

> *Now faith is the assurance of things hoped for,*
> *the conviction of things not seen. (Hebrews 11:1*
> *NASB)*

My patience grew weak. I wanted to be a priority to Ryan and not a burden or convenience like it appeared I was. I wanted Ryan and me to be "us" again instead of what we had become. I missed the smile on his face that let me know he was happy being with me. I wanted the communication we shared back when we dated... I wanted Ryan to be who I fell in love with.

I reminded Ryan of the counsel from the priest that if it's not God we find our security in, the walls that we find security in and cling to will come crumbling down, and we'll get crushed if we don't get out of the way. I shared also that a marriage won't grow by clinging to fear and to one's past instead of trust in our Lord.

The encouragement I used seemed to have led to a greater distance between Ryan and me and may have been the cause for him to flee and withdraw completely. Guilt and sorrow set in my spirit as I sat without my husband. It seemed to me that he viewed our marriage as a division between us rather than the blending we hoped it would be.

I continued to reach out to the pastor, the priest, and my counselor for help. The dreams Ryan and I used to talk nonstop about seemed lost. But I continued to pray, keeping hope and faith that I would witness a miracle in my marriage.

Feeling encouraged by *Matthew 6:33 (NLT), "Seek the Kingdom of God above all else, and live righteously, and he will give you everything you need,"* I held on to the God I knew to be faithful to His Word.

I waited with a hopeful heart to hear from Ryan. Every day felt like a new day filled with anticipation that today would be the day my marriage would turn around. At the end of the day, I went to bed brokenhearted without change. Still, tomorrow was a new day to unfold, and anything was possible.

> *With man this is impossible, but with God all things are possible. (Matthew 19:26 NIV)*

Spring arrived and so did my birthday. I was touched by my daughter's thoughtfulness with a necklace she picked out on her own. It was a cross with footprints imprinted on it to remind me that I'm not alone in my struggle…how precious and fitting.

That Mother's Day, Brad extended an invitation for me to join Eric, Jenna, and him for a trip to Alaska that his hunters, who I had known from being a part of the business, planned for Eric when he graduated. The trip was still months away, but knowing Eric and Jenna would want me to join them and not wanting to miss an opportunity to spend time with them, I accepted the invitation despite what others may think.

It had been months at this time since I last saw Ryan. My son's graduation was one week away. I wished for Ryan to be by my side for the occasion. I called him to ask if he still loved me. His response was, "Yes." I was hopeful that he would forgive me for being impatient in the past and consider joining me for Eric's graduation. My invitation for him to join me was declined. I accepted Ryan's response. When asked what I can do to help, he appeared uncertain.

I wondered if Ryan was so downcast that he felt unworthy of asking for anything. I wondered if I'd ever see him again or if he wanted to see me. I wondered if he missed me. Perhaps he thought I was too hard on him by suggesting for him to step up and be what God wanted him to be. I reassured Ryan of my love and that I'd be praying for him. I continued to hope, trust, and wait; I prayed for strength.

> *But they that wait upon the LORD shall renew their strength; they shall mount up with wings as eagles; they shall run, and not be weary; and they shall walk, and not faint. (Isaiah 40:31 KJV)*

Eric, Lauren, Jenna, and I went back to our hometown for my nephew's graduation. Had we not moved away, this would have been the class Eric would have graduated with. Our hometown graduations always felt sentimental to me. I suppose because of the closeness of everybody knowing everybody. To no surprise, the ceremony was emotional, not just for me, but for Eric too; I could tell by the tears in his eyes. I missed home and wondered if we ever should have left. I wondered if Eric regretted the move. I wondered if he would have continued sports and playing the drums like he enjoyed with his friends from the school he left behind. I'm most certain he would have as he enjoyed those activities a great deal. Then I thought of Lauren, whom my son adored and met in the town we currently lived; perhaps it all happened the way it was supposed to.

A smile came to my face as the class video played on the screen with my son included in the pictures. My eyes filled with tears again when the graduates hugged their parents and loved ones as they handed them a flower in appreciation. I always liked that part of the graduation ceremonies in my hometown. Unexpectedly, our good friend, Kendra, who always hung out with us back home, walked up and gave each of us a hug. We all had tears in our eyes at that moment. I missed Kendra and many things about what had been home to me for many years.

> If you want to know where your heart is,
> look to where your mind goes when it wanders.
> (Unknown Author)

Eric graduated the following weekend. For eighteen years, I dreaded that day and tried to prepare myself. I still wasn't ready and certain I'd never be. Knowing, though, that I still had my son home for the summer helped me get through the ceremony. I admired him walking across the stage to receive his diploma in his cap and gown. I was proud of Eric and honored to call him mine.

We came back to our house for the reception where family and friends gathered for lunch. Eric took me inside, handed me a rose, and embraced me with a hug. I love that boy of mine. He knew I'd love the gesture of the rose in appreciation of what our relationship meant to each other. I cried, but tears of gratitude for being blessed with the children I was given.

The following day Eric got dressed to take Lauren out for supper. I asked what the occasion was. "The twenty-first," he said. Like Ryan and I, Eric and Lauren met on the twenty-first of the month. Both of us couples acknowledged that day every month. I looked down wondering if Ryan and I would ever celebrate the twenty-first together again and cried, "It's my twenty-first too." Not knowing the words to lift my spirit, Eric wrapped his arms around me from behind and gave me a hug. Just knowing he cared gave me strength.

I longed so much for Ryan to hold me and tell me we were going to be all right. I longed to know what was on his heart. I felt sad that he seemed to have lost interest in pursuing our relationship and showing his love. I felt helpless as far as building our marriage.

I tried to keep from crying as best I could in front of my children; instead, I fought to keep a smile on my face and enjoy what God gave me. I tried to keep from crying in front of my parents as well. I didn't want my children or my parents concerned or hurting for me, so I stood strong with my head held high and kept my faith in God to come through for me again and carry me through the storm. There were moments, however, like that day on the twenty-first, that I couldn't keep from falling.

> We all have moments of weakness. It's how
> we recover from them that really counts. (Richelle
> Mead)

Perhaps you have an aching in your heart for a desire. Turn to our Lord, my friend, and trust that He cares.

I took in as much time as possible that summer with Eric before he would head off for college. On Memorial weekend, I enjoyed the day spent at the park riding bike and playing a game of mini-golf with him, Lauren, her dad, and Jenna. After that, we enjoyed a cookout together. Days like that lifted my spirits and gave me reason to be thankful. It also helped that I put my energy into prayer, meditation, and writing. It offered healing, comfort, and inspiration for me.

Eric helped his dad on the farm that summer. There were times that Jenna, Lauren, and I traveled out to the farm to hang out with him. While we visited, we did some cleaning for Brad and took in one of our favorite activities, four-wheel riding. Being at the farm where I raised Eric and Jenna brought back fond memories for me. To me, there's no place like the country. We then visited my mom and dad in the evening and spent an overnight at their house. The girls and I cuddled in one bed and giggled and talked until we got sleepy and fell asleep. Those were enjoyable moments.

Our hometown celebrated its Quasi Centennial that summer. Eric and Lauren, Jenna, her friends, Harley and Brooke, and I attended the celebration. It was good to see friends and acquaintances I hadn't seen in years, and having my children and friends along to experience the occasion too. We spent the night in my sister, Mary's camper on her farm and went swimming just like old times. I was thankful for these opportunities God led me to in the midst of my struggle. I wanted Ryan to be a part of my life, but while he wasn't, God continued to bless me through the storm.

> Strive toward what's ahead, but learn to thrive in the season you're currently in. (Nicki Koziarz)

My trip to Alaska with my children and their dad was approaching. It was supposed to be a surprise that I was going with, but I didn't quite manage to keep it a surprise. I purchased two pair of hiking boots, one for Eric and one for Jenna. Later, I went back to the store to purchase another pair for myself without my children knowing. I put the empty boxes in the dumpster outside thinking my children wouldn't notice. Eric, who's very observant, asked why there are three instead of two boxes in the garbage. I was busted since I wasn't quick to give a reasonable response. Eric gave a big old grin. I said we'd have to keep it a secret from his sister that I was going along.

I failed with that too, but not intentionally. I sent my friend, Kelly, a text that I was excited to be going to Alaska in a couple of days with my children and then mindlessly handed my phone to Jenna for her help. Even more mindlessly, I asked, "Who told you?" when Jenna screamed, "You're going with to Alaska!"

"You did," she said, "in your text to Kelly!"

Jenna was excited! I was too! We started packing right away and by the time her brother arrived home from work, the suitcases were scattered about.

"I take it the surprise got out?" Eric asked with a grin.

A couple of days later, after celebrating Eric's nineteen birthday, my children, their dad, Lauren, and I boarded the plane for our trip to Alaska which was meant to celebrate Eric's high school graduation. We stayed in a cabin near the Kenai River, owned by a kind hunter, Bruce, whom I was fortunate to meet while operating the hunting lodge with Brad while we were married.

The scenery was breathtaking and the weather just right with temps in the seventies most of the days. We indulged in the long daylight hours back at the cabin with fishing for salmon, chopping wood for a late-night campfire, and four-wheeling after taking in the sights during the day.

Halibut fishing on the North Pacific Ocean on the Gulf of Alaska off a boat house was one of the highlights. Jenna caught the first and biggest halibut, weighing in at eighty pounds! That was some fish! Riding on a horse trail, overlooking the beautiful scenery, walking along the ocean, and hiking a trail were some other highlights we enjoyed. While there, Jenna got to celebrate her fourteenth birthday; I was thankful to be invited on the trip. Memories that were made will last forever.

I will praise God's name in song and glorify
him with thanksgiving. (Psalm 69:30 NIV)

POINTS TO PONDER

Do you feel pressured to "settle" because you feel you are a burden otherwise?

It's easy to fear in our hearts that we are a burden when we don't feel valued. Friend, know that you are never a burden to our Lord. He has a purpose for your life.

For we are God's handiwork, created in Christ
Jesus to do good works, which God prepared in
advance for us to do. (Ephesians 2:10 NIV)

Is your heart aching for something? If so, to where do you turn for comfort and strength?

God is our refuge and strength, an ever-present
help in trouble. (Psalm 46:1 NIV)

Prayer: Almighty God, You are the Giver of all good. Thank You that You are all knowing, loving, and powerful. Thank You for the many gifts You have given to me and for the blessings upon my life. Forgive me please, for my moments of weakness when I am faced with a struggle. Thank You for carrying me when the struggle becomes too difficult for me to walk on my own. Help me, Jesus, to appreciate all You have given and to look to You for my refuge and strength. I pray this in Your holy name, Jesus. Amen.

Chapter 12

Embrace

EMBRACE

Consider it pure joy, my brothers and sisters, whenever you face trials of many kinds, because you know that the testing of your faith produces perseverance. Let perseverance finish its work so that you may be mature and complete, not lacking anything.

—James 1:2–4 (NIV)

After settling in back home, I gave my circumstance with my marriage some thought. Wondering how long the struggle would go on, I asked God for an answer to my on-going situation. God revealed to my heart that when I get angry at my husband, it is really Him that I am complaining about and putting down. He reminded me that He works in His time, not ours, that He knows what is best for us and when the time is right to give what we need. He will not be a moment too late.

> *The Lord is not slow in keeping his promise, as some understand slowness. Instead he is patient with you, not wanting anyone to perish, but everyone to come to repentance. (2 Peter 3:9 NIV)*

Willing to do what God wanted of me, I repented and asked what to do. I believed God revealed His answer through my devotion in *Jesus Calling*, by Sarah Young, that I took my eyes off Him and complained, got angry, felt impatient, and did not trust that He was working in ways I could not see. It read: *When you feel some lack, it is because you are not connecting with Me at a deep level. I offer abundant Life; your part is to trust Me, refusing to worry about anything. The only remedy is to switch your focus from the problem to My Presence.*

Encouraged to keep my eyes focused on God and inspired to attack the problem and not Ryan, the words from *1 Corinthians 13:4–8 (NIV)* came to my mind: *"Love is patient, love is kind. It does not envy, it does not boast, it is not proud. It does not dishonor others, it is not self-seeking, it is not easily angered, it keeps no record of wrongs. Love does not delight in evil, but rejoices with the truth. It always protects, always trusts, always hopes, always perseveres. Love never fails."*

I searched my heart and reflected on how I demonstrated unconditional love toward Ryan. I had not been patient and kind, but rather I was easily angered. I called Ryan to tell him I was sorry for being impatient while he tried sorting through his struggle. He accepted my apology, but I sensed that he may have been reluctant to trust me to be patient with him.

We agreed to see each other not long after our conversation. I didn't know what to expect, for three months had passed since we last saw each other. Nor did I know where to start putting pieces back together. We talked, but not about our dreams like we used to. I didn't know how to help Ryan deal with what seemed to hold him back.

After being with each other that weekend, we agreed to spend weekends together again. It looked as though weekends were all I was going to have with Ryan. I wanted more, but if I wanted to keep my marriage, I would have to make do with what I had at the time.

Call upon Me in the day of trouble; I shall rescue you; and you will honor Me. (Psalm 50:15 NASB)

With summer winding down, I needed to prepare my heart for what it had been dreading since the day Eric was born. Eric was enrolled for college at a nearby university just two hours away for a four-year program in Agronomy and Animal Science. I was happy for him to get to experience college and looked forward to hearing stories about his experience. But oh, how I'd miss my son who has been an inspiration since the moment I laid eyes on him while holding him in my arms for the first time.

More than anyone, Eric encouraged me and helped me through the storms in my life. He was a constant in my life daily that I could count on. I wasn't sure who I'd lean on for support while he was away, but I didn't want him to miss opportunities that life had to offer. It was important for me to trust our Lord to provide and give me strength for this too.

> *The LORD is my strength and my shield; my heart trusts in him, and he helps me. (Psalm 28:7 NIV)*

Eric told me when he was a little boy that my hugs felt like Jesus when I hugged him. What a sweet compliment to be compared to Jesus. I shared the same about Eric. His embrace was like resting in the arms of Jesus…a soothing comfort. He reassured me those hugs would never end, that he and I will never drift apart, that he would be home on the weekends and back after college. Just like I meant what I said when I made a promise to my children, I believed my son would also be true to his promises.

It helped that I got to be there to tour the college with Eric when he was making plans to prepare, and that I was with him on the day he got settled in. The campus at the university was beautiful and had so much to offer. I teased him that it was like a resort with everything he needed. He didn't think he was going to enjoy college quite that much, but it sure looked like a nice place to enjoy while studying.

Moving him into the dorm was an enjoyable day. We shopped for last minute items that we had forgotten, giggled over little things he might experience, and got to meet his roommate, John, who came across as a perfect match for Eric. My heart was at peace that Eric would be safe and happy at college.

Everything went as good as could be expected until we started heading toward the vehicle to make our "goodbyes." A "sick to my stomach" feeling came over me. Oh goodness; my heart fell like it's never fallen before. I embraced Eric with tears I couldn't control and hung on tighter than I ever have.

> Sometimes love means letting go, when you
> want to hold tighter. (Author unknown)

The tears wouldn't quit. I cried all the way home and when Jenna and I got home, I cried more. It seemed my son went from a baby in my arms to a man in the blink of an eye.

"Wow," Jenna said, "this is really hard, huh?"

"Goodbye is the hardest," I responded.

"At least you still have me," she said.

Jenna was right. Eric was away and I didn't have my husband, but yes, I had her. Unlike Eric though, Jenna was most often with a friend or at practice of some sort with the sports she was involved in. It wasn't going to be same without the hugs, words of encouragement, and kind gestures that Eric so readily offered when I was in need. I prayed, oh how I prayed for God's strength to help me through that emotional experience.

> *The LORD is my rock, and my safe place, and the One Who takes me out of trouble. My God is my rock, in Whom I am safe. He is my safe-covering, my saving strength, and my strong tower. (Psalm 18:2 NLV)*

The first time Jenna and I drove back to our hometown during the week for Jenna's visit with her dad without Eric along, it hit me that not only would I miss Eric being home during the week, but I'd miss him on our drives to visit his dad and my parents. It was he and

I that did most of the talking since Jenna was usually in the back seat listening to music.

I called Eric to tell him something was missing on the way out to his dad's place and that it was him. He said he knows it hurts, but that everything will be okay. It didn't feel like it was going to be okay.

During the drive, Jenna shared that it felt like she lost her dad when her brother left for college. I shared that it felt like I lost my companion, my big brother, and my son all at once when he left. Eric filled a lot of roles for his sister and me.

The visit with Jenna was surprisingly very nice. It helped to share what my heart was feeling. When we got home, she expressed that she was appreciative of the time she and I had alone in the car that evening. It made me feel good that she appreciated the time just she and I had. In fact, I used to feel badly that Jenna and I never had the opportunity for just the two of us being together like Eric and I had five years before she came along. I realized that without my husband and my son at home, Jenna and I would have an opportunity to have time together that I always wished we had. Perhaps Eric was right that everything was going to be okay. The bonding between Jenna and me helped take my mind off missing him.

He gives power to the weak and strength to the powerless. (Isaiah 40:29 NLT)

As it turned out, Jenna and I got busy with school back in session. She was in the eighth grade and still attending the middle school where I was the secretary. I was busy taking her to and from practices and attending her volleyball matches after work. I also got used to a new routine with just her and me. We had more visiting time since it was just the two of us. We stayed up late, sitting in her bedroom talking about everything from childhood memories, to her friends and sports she was involved with and boys, since she was getting to the age of noticing them. I loved our visits and the way we shared so carefree and easily with each other. I looked forward to the end of my workday and bonding more and more with her. Our trips back to her dad and my parents together were enjoyable as well. We never seemed to run out of conversation.

I also looked forward to Friday afternoons when Eric came home for the weekend. I enjoyed listening to him with a smile on his face as he shared stories about dorm life with the friends he made. My mom always told me she liked Eric's smile and the way it lit up the room. She was right. Eric has a smile that lights up the room. I could tell by the way Eric shared that he enjoyed college and making friends. He deserved to be happy. He still invited me to join him and Lauren for activities which I appreciated, and his hugs were even more special to me.

As far as my marriage, nothing changed except that a year had gone by since my wedding. I joined Ryan for an out of town work convention of his on the weekend of our first wedding anniversary. Ryan surprised me with the master suite. It had a balcony with the bedroom and master bathroom upstairs overlooking the dining room and living room below. While he attended his meetings, I took advantage of my alone time and enjoyed writing. I indulged also relaxing in a bubble bath with music playing, pretending to be living out my dream as a writer in my beautiful home in the country until my husband arrived home.

Since Ryan's meeting continued into the evening on Saturday, I used the hotel shuttle to go to church to attend the early Mass. The priest who did the service was the priest who instructed Ryan and me with marriage preparation when planning our wedding.

When the service was over, the priest offered to give me a ride back to the hotel for a chance to visit. He then invited to take Ryan and me out for supper for our anniversary to which Ryan agreed and appeared comfortable until the conversation turned to our marriage. It appeared to me that Ryan wanted to stay in his environment where he felt safe. It seemed he had no intent to make any changes regarding our marriage. I felt a sinking feeling in my spirit and felt sad.

The remainder of our evening back at the hotel was quiet as was the drive back to my house the following day. Ryan kissed me goodbye when we arrived at my house and headed back to his house from there.

Ryan's sensitivity that I fell in love with when we met concerned me at this point despite my attempts to be patient and not complain. It seemed as though it created hopelessness in his spirit.

I called on God for wisdom and guidance. As I rested in the stillness of His presence, He seemed to speak in love to my heart that it wasn't my job to fix Ryan, but to trust Him to do His work in His time. I did what I knew to do, continue to pray and hope for a miracle.

I admit there were moments during my struggle that I wondered what would have become of Michael and me had we not lived so many miles apart. Why my heart still felt a connection with Michael thirteen years after meeting him, I wasn't sure... I may never know the answer to my question. All I could do was give my circumstance to God and trust that He would lead me in the direction to go.

My attention was drawn to a poem by an unknown author hanging on my refrigerator, *Let Go and Let God* that was given to me several years back at a church retreat. The poem describes a person bringing their broken dreams to the Lord. But instead of leaving Him in peace to work alone, they tried to help with ideas of their own. After getting frustrated, they snatched their dreams back and complained that God was too slow. God replied, "My child, what could I do? You never did let go."

Do I let go of my husband in order for God to do His work in our marriage? I wondered. I didn't want to give up on my marriage or on Ryan. But perhaps being willing to let go was all I could do.

The following weekend, I left Ryan a note before I left for the church service on Sunday morning, telling him I was done fighting for him to stay and that it was his choice to stay or to go. When I returned home, Ryan and his bags were gone. I sat down and cried not knowing if what I had done would rekindle the dreams he and I once shared or make matters worse for our marriage. It was my hope that Ryan would have stayed and proved his love for me.

Several days later, I received an email from Ryan. He was counseling and asked for me to join him. I hoped his counselor would have an answer for our marriage. She, like my counselor, the priest, and the pastor, suggested that Ryan fight for his marriage and let go of what was holding him back.

The silence in the room was answer enough. I couldn't control what I couldn't control. With that being said, I stepped out of the way, let go of what I had no control over, and gave control to the One who could complete what had been started.

> *And I am sure of this, that he who began a*
> *good work in you will bring it to completion at the*
> *day of Jesus Christ. (Philippians 1:6 ESV)*

I can tell you, I wasn't expecting to be where I was and wasn't sure where to go from there. All communication between Ryan and I was cut off. I wanted to believe there was reason for hope in the midst of my struggle and a lesson to be learned. I trusted with what faith I had and prayed beauty would come from the ashes of my heartache.

Are you in a situation that you need to surrender to God in order to let Him do His work?

While I waited in faith for God to do His work, I embraced my circumstance and enjoyed what blessings I had been given. God continued to bless my family and me in ways I never expected. As volleyball season began to wind down, Jenna wanted to try out for gymnastics, a sport she wanted to participate in from an early age, but wasn't given the opportunity because I was hesitant. After learning more about the sport, I finally agreed for Jenna to give gymnastics a try.

With space being limited and more athletes trying out than there was room for on the team, I prepared myself for the possibility of Jenna not making the team since she hadn't any experience. She was the last of the girls to visit with the coaches the evening the team was selected. I waited patiently outside the room and watched the girls who made the team give their mom a high five. Others displayed a look of disappointment. At last Jenna came out with a blank look on her face. Remaining silent until we reached the car, I waited for the results. As it turned out, Jenna wasn't selected for middle school gymnastics. "Better yet," she said, "I made junior varsity!"

I was proud of Jenna and thankful for her good news. I admired her spirit that anything was possible.

> As you think, so shall you be. (Dr. Wayne
> W. Dyer)

Meanwhile at college, Eric became a member of the Farmhouse Fraternity whose motto is: "Builder of Men." To be a member of the Farmhouse Fraternity was a privilege as standards and requirements were expected. I felt honored to attend the ceremony prepared for Eric and his "brothers" to be inducted into the organization. It was truly a pleasure to witness the fine man my son was growing into. I was immensely proud of him too.

I enjoyed heart to heart talks with Eric on the weekends while we prepared meals sampling his recipes from his home economics class in high school and recipes from home. I felt grateful to have him cooking with me in the kitchen, hanging out with him and Lauren, and having him stand next to his sister and me in church on Sundays. God was good to me in so many ways!

> A mother's greatest masterpiece is her chil-
> dren. (Unknown Author)

A celebration was planned for my mom and dad's sixtieth wedding anniversary. Of course, I wished that Ryan would have joined my children and me, but I didn't let it show that I was missing him. I presented myself with confidence like everything was okay. Jenna shared that she didn't like that I pretended to be happy and have it all together. I didn't like pretending either, but pitying myself wasn't going to get me anywhere. I assured Jenna that I may not have everything I wanted, but what I had was worth more than I lacked. I had her and her brother there to celebrate the long life of my mom and dad still together. I was thankful for my relationship with all of them and for their support and encouragement.

The truth was that I had more than most have and even though I was very grateful for what I had, it was hard at times not to fall into the pit of self-pity. I missed hearing Ryan's voice over the phone before I went to sleep every night. I missed his email messages several times a day. I missed being with him, being in his arms, and talking about the dreams we shared. Still, I had a grateful heart for what I had been blessed with and hope in my spirit that God would use my situation for good.

My mom, too, was bothered. She commented that she didn't understand why I was going through what I went through, that she struggled to watch me pretend that everything was well with me, and that there wasn't a day that went by that she and Dad didn't pray for me. I appreciated my mom and dad's prayers. I explained to Mom that I believed I was being prepared for a calling to teach of God's goodness and mercy. That's what gave me strength to keep in faith and continue my journey.

> *You intended to harm me, but God intended it all for good. He brought me to this position so I could save the lives of many people. (Genesis 50:20 NLT)*

The pastor who Ryan and I met with numerous times kept in contact to help me stay in faith. I admired the passion in him to encourage and inspire me to keep hope alive. I was grateful for him in my life.

I spent Thanksgiving thankful to be with family, wishing still that I would have heard from Ryan. I tried not to dwell, though, on what was lacking and to be grateful instead for my many blessings. One of which was getting to go Black Friday shopping the following day with Eric. He shared that he believed Ryan to be a good man who needed my understanding. Jenna agreed, for she understood also that I'd want understanding if I was in Ryan's position.

Wanting to reach out to Ryan to offer understanding, I sent him an email to wish him and his family a Happy Thanksgiving and to let him know they were in my prayers. It seemed that Ryan reached a low point in his life. He responded to my message expressing shame and hopelessness as to where he was emotionally. From what it appeared, Ryan lost hope to fight for our marriage. Though I felt helpless not having control over my circumstance, I clung to my belief that God would use my circumstance for His purpose for me, to glorify Him and spread His goodness to others in need.

> *For the earth shall be filled with the knowl-edge of the glory of the LORD, as the waters cover the sea. (Habakkuk 2:14 NIV)*

POINTS TO PONDER

Are you struggling to surrender a situation or circumstance to God that you have been praying about?

Friend, God cares about the details in your life. He knows the hurt your heart is suffering. He will make good on His promise to use your circumstance and bring triumph from the trial. Take comfort in trusting that our Lord is in control. Embrace your blessings, let go of your circumstances, and give all of them to God.

> *With your whole being you embrace God set-ting things right, and then you say it, right out loud: "God has set everything right between him and me!" Scripture reassures us, "No one who trusts God like this—heart and soul—will ever regret it." (Romans 10:10–11 MSG)*

Prayer: Dear Lord, thank You for the many blessings in my life. Open my eyes to the ways I'm relying on my own efforts rather than putting my trust in You. Help me to embrace the current situation I am experiencing and to rely on You no matter the circumstance. Thank You for caring about all the details in my life and for keeping Your promises. Forgive me please, for the times I have taken what I have been given for granted and for the times I have gotten frustrated or impatient and not given complete control of my life to You. Thank You for using my circumstance to prepare me for Your purpose. Help me to surrender what only You can fix, to embrace my blessings and all what You have allowed in my life, and to give You complete control to do Your work in Your time. I pray this in Your precious name, Jesus. Amen.

Chapter 13

GOD LOVES

*Love bears all things, believes all things, hopes
all things, endures all things.*

—1 Corinthians 13:7 (ESV)

I prayed for God to show me what to do. It didn't seem right that neither my husband nor I fight for our marriage. I found encouragement that day through one of my daily devotions to have courage and trust. I was uncertain, though, for what I was supposed to have courage. I asked God if He wanted me to have courage to file for a divorce and trust that Ryan would take a stand.

"Have courage and trust," was all the response it felt in my spirit that I received.

About that time, a new song, "Need You Now," by Plumb, came out on the Christian K-love radio station that my heart resonated with. It's a song about someone in a difficult circumstance that's afraid, tired of holding on, wondering how they got where they are, and needing healing and hope to believe that there's beauty and a reason for the pain they are experiencing. It's about trying to hear that still, small voice and confessing to God that He is needed for continued strength. I cried out to God and prayed that He would have mercy on me, give me strength to get through my storm, and guide me where to go.

Jenna reminded me of Pastor Joel Osteen's encouragement that another day of my struggle was one day closer to my dream. It was of course encouragement to be reminded that my dream was another day closer.

While I waited for God to answer, I recalled the words of advice from a friend, Bonnie, "If you don't know what to do, don't do anything until you know what the right thing is to do."

The advice given by my friend calmed my spirit. For if we don't know what to do, then it makes sense that the answer is to be still and wait after we've prayed until we learn or are told what to do… I prayed, waited, and watched for God to guide me.

Christmas was just a couple of days away. The owner, Bill, from the lodge that I managed, who became a dear friend of mine, invited me out for lunch. Being aware that Ryan and I were separated, he suggested for me to reach out to Ryan by baking him cookies and delivering them to his house for Christmas.

His suggestion was very thoughtful; however, I didn't follow through with it. I was hurt from feeling neglected and wanted Ryan to be the one to reach out.

Perhaps you're being prompted to go out of your way to do something nice for someone, but for reasons you find justifiable, you resist as well.

While continuing to seek God's will, wondering whether to file for a divorce, God revealed in my heart a feeling that my motive for filing for a divorce demonstrated control rather than love. It was the truth. The only reason I considered a divorce was to push Ryan into committing to our marriage.

Taking into consideration what God revealed, I contacted the pastor I had been visiting with for counsel. He advised that Ryan appeared to be struggling at the time and may very well give up on our marriage if I filed for a divorce. The pastor agreed that my motive for filing for a divorce seemed that of control rather than love. He encouraged instead that I that pay Ryan a visit like Bill suggested.

Chatter filled my thoughts to keep my guard up and not risk getting hurt some more. I believed that if I reached out to Ryan, I'd be sending the message that I was okay with feeling neglected. That wasn't okay with me though. I was angry over feeling neglected and didn't want to continue feeling that way.

Christmas vacation arrived. Eric was home from college for a few weeks and Jenna and I had a break from school. I started my break off by spending time in church at the chapel to seek what God wanted me to do. His whisper grew louder in my spirit for me to have courage and trust.

"Have courage in what, God?" I prayed.

While continuing to wait for God to come through, I longed for a break from dwelling on my circumstance. I wished to get away with my children, but lacked extra income at the end of the month for such things as a vacation. I prayed God might provide financially for something special to do with my children to lighten the spirits of all of us.

My children and I celebrated Christmas by going to Christmas Eve Mass together with Lauren, exchanging presents, having an evening meal, and watching a movie. The following day we drove back to our hometown for Christmas with family, including Eric and Jenna's dad. We spent an overnight with my mom and dad which was a treat for my parents as well as for me.

On the drive back to our house, Eric reminded me of all the crying and worrying I did when he left for college and there we were still hanging out just like he said we would. Yes, all had gone well just like Eric said it would and the school year was already half over. I certainly was thankful for the time my children spent with me. I enjoyed that ride with both Eric and Jenna just like old times.

After totaling up the money I received for Christmas, along with a bonus from Bill, I had enough to pay for the presents I bought for my family and enough left over to take my children out of town to go skiing. My children were in awe of God's goodness; they knew I prayed for financial blessing to take a trip. I assured them, "When you turn to God in prayer, never doubt His faithfulness to answer."

With all the prayers they saw God answer already, they agreed.

You faithfully answer our prayers with awesome deeds, O God our Savior. (Psalm 65:5 NLT)

After Christmas had passed, Eric, Lauren, Jenna, her best friend, Brooke, who joined us often, and I packed our bags to spend a couple of days with Lauren's brother and family to go skiing for a day.

Surprisingly, my skiing skills improved greatly compared to the first time I gave it a try, five years earlier with my ex-fiancé, Robert, and Eric, Jenna, and Brooke. It was an experience I'll never forget. I stayed on the bunny hill the entire first day of skiing. Eric was caring and patient. He stuck with me up to the point that I got tricked on day two by one of the employees at the ski resort to ride the chair lift with him to a beginner's path when Eric left my side momentarily. To Eric's surprise, I came tumbling with my skis to the bottom of the hill, shouting, "That was fun!" while he was searching to see where I went.

I explained that the man on the bunny hill showed me a much slower, safer path. To my astonishment, I learned it was the same path everyone else had been taking, including Jenna and Brooke who were only ten years old at that time. I don't like getting tricked into things, but in this case it was a good lesson for me…and fun!

Little did I know, I was in for another surprise experience during this trip too, my second time skiing. I was having a great time, thanks to Eric and Lauren for sharing their chair lift with me and making sure I didn't get left behind.

After several trips up the chair lift, I happened to notice a lady at the bottom of the lift looking as though she had her eye on me. I had this feeling she wanted to grab my chair just as I got off. I wondered how she planned to get on my chair though, because the lift moves quickly and waits for no one.

I wasn't wrong. That lady sure did want my seat and attempted to get it! In the process, I got knocked to the ground before I had a chance to get off on my own. And while struggling to get up without embarrassing myself too much, I got plowed into by the person on the next chair and got knocked to the ground again!

Oh dear, I thought, *I must look a sight!*

There was no time to waste. I had to get myself out of the way before the person on the next lift knocked into me too and caused an even bigger scene. While tangled in my skis and attempting to crawl out of the way, I looked up at Eric and Lauren who were laughing hysterically. I imagine it did look funny!

Once I got to safety, Eric and Lauren, still laughing uncontrollably, explained what had happened. Apparently, the lady who wanted my seat wasn't quick enough to get on it after she plowed me off, so she knocked the person behind me off of their seat as well, who then landed on me while I was attempting to get up. Truthfully, I didn't mind my little mishap. I took in stride what happened and laughed it off.

I thought how Ryan and his daughter would have laughed hysterically as well with Eric and Lauren. I wished they would have been with us to enjoy what we enjoyed. I longed very much to be reunited with Ryan and to have the marriage we talked about having while we dated.

While heading back from our trip, the song, "Help Me Hold On," by Travis Tritt played on the radio. My heart softened from the words in the song—words I longed to hear from Ryan. I wished he would ask me to help him hold on to what we had like the artist sang. After arriving home, I dug out my Travis Tritt CD to listen to the song, "Help Me Hold On," and came across another favorite of mine, "Anymore," by Travis as well. Travis sang of a small voice repeating deep inside his soul expressing that he can't keep pretending he doesn't love a special someone anymore. The song made me realize God was speaking through my daughter during my mom and dad's anniversary celebration when she shared that she didn't like seeing me pretending to be strong and acting as though I didn't need love.

I didn't want to keep hiding behind the wall I built to protect my heart and pretend I didn't love Ryan anymore. I loved him and wanted forgiveness between us. I wished so much for him to reach out and ask me to help him hold on to the love we had.

New Year's Eve was spent cooking supper with Eric and Lauren and sitting around the kitchen table sharing stories with them and Jenna. God gave me an amazing gift when He gave my son and daughter to me to love and care for, but also one in my son's girlfriend who allowed me to be a part of her life with Eric. Lauren's willingness meant more to me than she will ever know.

The following day, I built up the courage to visit Ryan's mom and dad and share with them how much I missed their son. I had hoped perhaps they would have an influence on Ryan's decision to act on our marriage. As much as they wanted Ryan and me together however, they had no control either. I turned from my stubbornness and reached out to Ryan as well that day. I sent him an email. He responded, but again with what seemed to me a spirit of hopelessness. My heart felt abandoned. *If only my husband would open his heart to the love I wanted to give*, I thought. *If only he'd see the good that would come if he embraced what God offered.*

Believing still that God wanted to bring good out of my circumstance, I knelt in prayer seeking discernment of what to do and for the strength to do it. Still hearing God's whisper in my spirit, "Have courage and trust," I asked if I was supposed to have courage and trust that Ryan would take a stand to our marriage if I requested a divorce.

I was scared. I believed the pastor was right. Ryan was possibly so troubled that he may have been in agreement to file for a divorce without fighting for our marriage; I was terrified as well that if I visited him, he would reject me.

I turned to the pastor for insight as to what I should do. The pastor encouraged me to keep holding on, for when the Lord tests us, He often pushes us to our limits.

> *But God is faithful; He will not suffer you to*
> *be tempted beyond that which ye are able to bear,*
> *but with the temptation will also make a way to*

escape, that ye may be able to bear it. (1 Corinthians 10:13 KJ21)

The pastor reassured that times of testing bring blessings if we remain in faith and obey God.

Blessed is the man who remains steadfast under trial, for when he has stood the test he will receive the crown of life, which God has promised to those who love him. (James 1:12 ESV)

He encouraged me again to reach out to Ryan since it seemed he wouldn't be the one to make the first move, but to offer comfort and encouragement instead of a divorce. I found his insight to be inspiring, for the scripture in my daily devotion for that day was, *"We who are strong have an obligation to bear with the failings of the weak, and not to please ourselves" (Romans 15:1 ESV).*

With the insight I was offered, I believed God was calling me to be the one to reach out to Ryan and express forgiveness. Feeling somewhat reluctant yet, to forgive that is, I took to prayer all that was on my heart and asked God to lead me to do what was right.

Even if they sin against you seven times in a day and seven times come back to you saying, "I repent," you must forgive them. (Luke 17:4 NIV)

My daily devotion that next day encouraged forgiveness for anyone who has wronged another and for those who have been wounded to take the initiative to take the first step in showing love and acceptance.

They caused the first wound, but you are causing the rest; this is what not forgiving does. (Bryant McGill)

Later in the day while in the middle of my workout, the words, "Forgiveness is not excusing the wrong that someone has done, but letting go of the hurt that someone has caused and giving them another chance," came to me from out of the blue. Jenna assured me of her confidence that God placed those words upon my heart as an answer to my prayer and that His words speak truth. I knew what she said to be true. I gave thought to the words that came to my mind and looked at the meaning of forgiveness in a different light with a new perspective. My heart softened toward Ryan to forgive and reach out to him again.

Let us not become weary in doing good, for at the proper time we will reap a harvest if we do not give up. (Galatians 6:9 NIV)

POINTS TO PONDER

Is the Holy Spirit prompting your heart to do something that you doubt or perhaps even fear?

Perhaps the prompting is to forgive another, but you're resistant because you think the recipient is undeserving.

Dear one, there's power in the Holy Spirit's promptings. Don't let fear, a calloused heart, wrong motives, or even being weary stand in the way and hold you back from what God has in store for you or what He wants to teach you. Press on knowing that tomorrow you are another day closer to what God has in store for you.

All a person's ways seem pure to them, but motives are weighed by the LORD. (Proverbs 16:2 NIV)

Prayer: Thank You, Jesus, for Your love. You love me even when I don't deserve. Forgive me for the times I have chosen not to love or forgive another. Align my motives with Your Word and character and please help me to forgive and love others the way You forgive and love me. Help me please, to keep in mind that times of testing bring blessing. Help me, Jesus, to push through any fear or doubt that I may feel, to follow the promptings of the Holy Spirit, and to not get frustrated when I may feel weary from the ongoing storm. Help me also not to be afraid to be vulnerable, but rather to reach out for help by being honest with my feelings to others. I pray all of this in Your holy name, Jesus. Amen.

Chapter 14

HOPE

Rejoice in hope, be patient in tribulation, be constant in prayer.

—Romans 12:12 (ESV)

After my change of heart, I sent flowers to Ryan early in the morning for Valentine's Day with a card expressing forgiveness as well as my love for him. Later that day, I received a phone call from the flower shop in town letting me know they had a delivery to drop off for me if I was still at work.

Certain that the flowers on their way were from Ryan, I was hopeful that he accepted my apology and was willing to work through our circumstance. Upon reading the note attached to the flowers after they were delivered, my spirit turned from hope to disappointment. The flowers were not from my husband, but rather from my ex-husband wishing me a happy day.

I wasn't upset with Brad. It was kind of him to send me flowers. I was disappointed, however, for it appeared that Ryan didn't appreciate my act of kindness with the gift of flowers and heartfelt note I sent to him.

"Forgive him." I heard within my spirit.

Forgive him… Really? I retorted in my mind, *Could my husband not have acknowledged my gesture to reach out to him and show that I care?*

At that very moment, the words from *Luke 23:34 (NIV)* that Jesus spoke as He was dying on the cross, *"Father, forgive them, for they do not know what they are doing,"* came to me.

It was as though the Lord whispered in my spirit, "Find strength in Me." I hung my head in sorrow and regret for letting Jesus down. How quickly I allowed disappointment to set in my spirit so soon after my change of heart. I confessed my sin to God and asked for help to rise above my struggle and to be patient with a hopeful heart.

> *A new command I give you: Love one another.*
> *As I have loved you, so you must love one another.*
> *(John 13:34 NIV)*

That evening while Jenna and I were having supper, Jenna innocently asked, "So mom, what are you giving up for Lent this year?"

I hung my head and said, "Hmm…funny you should ask, because we are only into the second day of Lent and already, I have failed miserably."

Jenna, wise and intuitive like her brother, chuckled and said, "Let me guess, you gave up complaining."

I shamefully nodded. "Yes, and that's not all. I'm trying to work on loving unconditionally."

"You did blow it," she said with a grin and a light heart, "but tomorrow is a new day."

After weeks of hoping to hear from Ryan, he finally responded, this time expressing feelings of unworthiness. I sank into despair and was brokenhearted, for it looked as though Ryan utterly lost hope for our marriage to be restored.

Jenna encouraged me not to give up on my marriage even though it appeared as though Ryan had given up. I felt so helpless. I prayed and asked God how I can encourage my husband rather than discourage him…how I can build him up without him feeling torn down.

Sometimes all a loved one can do is sit quietly and pray with expectant faith that God is working through the storm. Ryan appeared to be at a place where only God's healing power could mend his broken heart. Our marriage would only be restored through the grace of God.

> *Now faith is the assurance of things hoped for, the conviction of things not seen. (Hebrews 11:1 ESV)*

It was spoken to me through devotion not to feel sorry for myself, but rather to be thankful for the storm as thankfulness awakens us to God's presence, which overshadows our struggles. *"Rejoice in the Lord always. Again I will say, rejoice! Let your gentleness be known to all men. The Lord is at hand. Be anxious for nothing, but in everything by prayer and supplication, with thanksgiving, let your requests be made known to God"* (Philippians 4:4–6 NKJV).

If you've been experiencing an ongoing crisis for some time already, you know how challenging it can be to keep hope when you feel helpless.

Later that winter, when I filed for my income taxes, I shared with my accountant that I was still separated as it made a difference on my tax return. My accountant shared a piece of advice once given to him that I found encouraging, "It's always too soon to ever give up."

I regretted not paying Ryan a visit over Christmas with baked cookies like my friend, Bill, suggested for me to do. I gave thought to going to see him for no reason other than showing my love and concern for him, but I feared he was so broken that he'd push me away.

Pastor Joel Osteen's encouraging words that week, "God puts circumstances into our lives so big that only He can make peace, healing, and good come out of it," offered hope for my circumstance that was out of my control. I believed good would come from this circumstance, too, as hurts from previous circumstances taught me valuable lessons and helped build my faith. I kept my trust in God that peace, healing, and good were on the way and that without the experience, I wouldn't learn what God wanted to teach me.

Continuing to stay in faith, I learned, is easier said than done. Though I struggled with keeping patient and continuing to keep hope during the trying time of being separated from Ryan, God was good to pour blessings along the way to lighten the load.

> *For I will pour water upon him that is thirsty, and floods upon the dry ground: I will pour my spirit upon thy seed, and my blessing upon thine offspring. (Isaiah 44:3 KJV)*

As Jenna's gymnastics season came to a close, she decided to join the track team that year. She believed she could do anything. "Why not me?" were her words of affirmation she claimed to be successful in track. I admired her confidence.

Setting her mind on excelling, Jenna surpassed the triple jump record that season at the middle school she attended, not by a couple of inches, but by over a foot. That was a proud moment for my daughter and me. Attending her meets and getting to know other parents helped keep my spirits high and my mind off my circumstance.

Needing all the encouragement I could get, I reconnected with my counselor that spring for advice on how I can be of help to Ryan and what I can do to help save our marriage. My counselor encouraged me with *Matthew 19:26 (NIV): "With man this is impossible, but with God all things are possible."* He often quoted as well, *"If God is for us, who can be against us?" (Romans 8:31 NIV), "But seek first his kingdom and his righteousness, and all these things will be given to you as well" (Matthew 6:33 NIV),* and *"No good thing does he withhold from those whose walk is blameless" (Psalm 84:11 NIV).*

My counselor stressed that as long as we put God first, we will be provided for and that God uses EVERYTHING, not just some things, for the good of us. I liked that encouragement.

> *And we know that all things work together for good to them that love God, to them who are called according to his purpose. (Romans 8:28 KJV)*

By this time, word got out to some that my marriage had been failing. My sister, Janet, shared what the talk back home was. I was criticized for staying married. I learned judgment exists no matter where we live and no matter if we do right or if we do wrong.

Jenna encouraged me with another one of Pastor Joel Osteen's teachings that it matters only how God looks at a situation and not how others look at it. She also encouraged me to stay true to my heart and reminded me that the bigger the problem, the bigger the blessing. I found encouragement through the inspiration Jenna offered and through scripture that my counselor often repeated. I was convinced that if I put first what I believed God wanted me to do, blessings would pour forth.

> *Instead of shame and dishonor, you will enjoy a double share of honor. You will possess a double portion of prosperity in your land, and everlasting joy will be yours. (Isaiah 61:7 NLT)*

Both the pastor I had been visiting with and my counselor assured me that if we are determined not to follow God's ways, we can expect trouble; even if we follow God's ways, there can be struggle. But if we stay in faith while in the midst of the storm, we can be assured that God will see us through and make us stronger and better people in the end. The pastor shared that God gave me an opportunity to put into practice what He has taught me. My counselor reminded me numerous times of my passion to teach of God's love and faithfulness. He'd encourage me by asking, "Who better to teach than the one who learned?"

> *May he equip you with all you need for doing his will. May he produce in you, through the power of Jesus Christ, every good thing that is pleasing to him. All glory to him forever and ever. Amen! (Hebrews 13:21 NLT)*

My counselor and the pastor were indeed a gift to me, especially in the time of my struggle. I was set on seeking God's will and not the will of others.

That year was the first that I didn't get to celebrate my birthday with both my son and daughter. It landed on a weekday while Eric was at college which was a little disheartening, but that didn't stop Jenna from making it special. She told me to dress up and surprised me with supper at a nice restaurant downtown where a table with flowers and a birthday balloon was reserved for us! That was sure a pleasant surprise and happy birthday!

About that time, I received an invitation through Proverbs 31 Ministry to attend a She Speaks Conference in North Carolina for writers or speakers. Believing I had a story to offer encouragement to stay in faith in times of struggles, I considered registering for the conference. Doubt, however, crept in almost immediately.

For starters, I lacked the means of finances to pay for such an event and secondly, I was frightened of traveling outside of my comfort zone by myself. And then there were the doubts of my abilities. Even though a voice within told me that others could learn from my experience, there was another voice that told me I was too insignificant to be the inspiration my heart desired. Anyway, my story was nowhere near completion, so I felt the timing just wasn't right.

Nonetheless, I prayed for God to lead me in the direction He wanted me to go.

> *I will instruct you and teach you in the way*
> *you should go; I will counsel you with my loving eye*
> *on you. (Psalm 32:8 NIV)*

While in church that weekend, I noticed a man and a woman sitting in front of my children and me. The man resembled Ryan which made me miss him dearly. I felt a tug on my heart to go and visit Ryan, but fear that he'd reject me continued to have a hold a me. My option then was to wait for Ryan to be willing to reach out to me.

When my children and I got into the car following the service, I shared that the man sitting in front of us reminded me of Ryan. "I miss Ryan," I said as I fought back tears. Sometimes there is nothing even a loved one can say to take one's hurt away. Jenna stayed silent. Eric offered a sympathetic gesture of his hand on my shoulder and sighed, "I know you do."

I prayed Ryan would reach out to me.

After arriving home from the church that same day, Bill, the owner of the lodge, called to check in and see how I was doing. I shared my interest in the She Speaks Conference, along with the reasons that it wasn't the right timing. Bill had already known of my passion to share my story and had been encouraging me for some time to write it. He wouldn't hear of me putting my dream on hold any longer and passing up the opportunity to attend the conference. He offered to help pay the expense, which I declined since there was still the concern of traveling alone.

Eric and Jenna overheard the conversation with Bill and encouraged me to accept. Jenna had become quite the inspiration ever since her brother was away at college. She spoke up and shouted, "YOLO, Mom!"

"What does YOLO mean?" I asked.

"You only live once," she said.

She saw the conference as an opportunity for my dream to come true. She encouraged me to turn my doubt to confidence and attend the conference as well as to accept my friend's offer to help me pay for it. She even had a solution for traveling arrangements. She said she and her dad could go with and make the trip into a vacation for the two of them while I attend the conference. I had to admit, I liked her positive thinking! What seemed impossible only minutes ago, turned into an opportunity for God to work a miracle. I accepted Bill's generous gift.

The following week, it seemed the sermon in church was meant specifically for me to hear. The priest shared how we are called to pick up our cross without complaining about our struggle and without pitying ourselves. We are to carry our cross with faith that God will use the struggle for good. And when we carry our cross in faith without complaining, we receive blessings that are worth the wait and effort. He reminded us to look to Jesus for strength to carry our cross and wait with hope for blessings, as Jesus blesses accordingly.

> *Be strong and courageous, for your work will*
> *be rewarded. (2 Chronicles 15:7 NLT)*

While at my next visit with my counselor, I was encouraged when he discussed *Genesis 18* where God promised a son to Sarah and Abraham though they were old in age. They had to endure the wait and keep faith and hope alive. God kept His word and made it so that Sarah and Abraham had a baby because they had kept their faith.

> *The Lord is faithful in all his words and gra-*
> *cious in all his actions. (Psalm 145:13 CSB)*

Sarah and Abraham's story reminded me of my sister, Kate, and her husband. They were married for over twenty years before they were blessed with a child. It was Kate's dream to be a mom, but to no avail, she and her husband struggled to conceive. Many had given up that Kate would have a baby, but she wouldn't take, "No" for an answer, for she believed God put that dream in her heart and so did I.

After much thought, prayer, and preparation, Kate and her husband opted for adoption. Still, years passed until one day Kate felt the Lord prompting her to prepare a room for her baby. She obeyed and painted a room fitting for a newborn. She then believed that God placed it upon her heart to purchase a crib. But every time she went to the store to purchase the crib, she backed out for fear that someone she knew would see her and question her purchase.

I reminded Kate of the story about Noah and the Ark in *Genesis 6:9–8:21*, where God had a plan for Noah just as He had one for her and her husband. Even though it may have seemed ridiculous for Noah to build an ark, Noah obeyed and built the ark exactly how God instructed him to do. God kept His word to save Noah and his family because Noah acted out of obedience.

I encouraged Kate to hold tight to her dream. I prayed she'd be a Noah and obey even if what God asked of her seemed ridiculous. I prayed that she would go back to the store to purchase what might be the only white crib left on the shelf.

Kate did it! She went to the store and couldn't believe her eyes. There was only one white crib left on the shelf. She mustered up the courage to put the crib into her cart and purchased it without running into a single person she knew.

Months passed with no sign of a baby on the way, but a room prepared and a crib waiting to be used. Like Noah, Kate believed the Lord spoke within her spirit and that it was only a matter of time before her dream came to pass despite what it seemed.

More time passed. Kate began to lose hope and wondered if there was really a baby on the way. She believed the Lord spoke again that she would have a Christmas baby. Her spirits lifted, but Christmas came and went with still no baby. After doubting again, she believed once more that the Lord spoke within her spirit, "Believe, you will have your baby soon."

Several more years passed with still no baby. Then the day came! In December, almost ten years later, Kate and her husband received a phone call that they were chosen to be the parents to a newborn baby girl, my niece and my goddaughter, Rylee!

Just like the flood arrived that God said would come, the baby that my sister was promised arrived as well. Kate learned not to doubt and to never give up on what God has promised. He showed her that obedience opens the door for blessings!

> *And as you have believed, so let it be done for you. (Matthew 8:13 NKJV)*

After six months had passed since I last saw Ryan, hope in my spirit began to diminish despite the encouraging reminder of Kate's story not to give up. I struggled after another disheartening weekend on a Monday to get through my workday. Doubt that I'd see Ryan again made me want very much to be at home by myself to wallow in self-pity instead of having to be at work. As soon as I walked through the door when I got home that day, I sat myself down and a flood of tears poured forth.

"What do I have to do to get through to my husband?" I cried.

Silence filled the room.

After a good cry, I pulled myself together and turned on the radio thinking God would come through in a song like He so often did. Not even my new favorite song, "Need You Now," that gave me strength to carry on, came on the radio. God remained silent.

I couldn't pick up the phone and call the pastor, for I had just spoken with him over the weekend and his last advice, which frightened me, was to go and visit Ryan. I couldn't call my mom or my sisters and cry because their advice also was to visit Ryan. Jenna was at track practice and Eric away at college. I sat there alone in self-pity, crying and desperate for the answer to my question.

Whatever it was, I decided that what God wanted to say was going to have to wait until I returned from my PTA meeting I had scheduled that evening, which I was not looking forward to because of my mood at the moment.

Luckily, the meeting was over quicker than usual, which meant I could pick Jenna up from her friend, Brooke's house and hear an encouraging word God may have placed upon her heart to say about my situation.

God had different plans however.

It all started with one of the PTA moms, Kristen, inquiring how marriage life was treating me.

"Good," I responded.

Kristen then asked how it was working out for Ryan to commute from my house to work an hour away. Not wanting to expose what was really happening, I explained that Ryan's house had not yet sold so he was still there for the time being. Upon learning that we lived in separate homes, Kristen asked how often Ryan and I got to see each other. Too ashamed to admit that my marriage was failing and wishing she hadn't been so curious, I fidgeted with my keys uncertain how to cover what I had been hiding.

Realizing I couldn't cover up with another lie, I looked into the faces of the PTA moms all waiting for an answer. I was exhausted from pretending that I was okay, when the truth was, I was hurting desperately on the inside. I broke into a sob, confessing that Ryan and I had been separated and hadn't seen each other in six months and I didn't know what to do anymore. The four women I had been meeting with every month for that school year had a look of shock on their faces upon hearing the unexpected news. As for me, a weight seemed to lift.

After offering their sympathy and having a better understanding of my circumstance, they suggested that I drive to see Ryan and assure him of my love. Overcome with such fear of rejection, I admitted, "I'm too afraid."

"What are you afraid of?" they asked.

"Rejection," I said.

I feared Ryan would tell me he doesn't want to stay married. There'd be no reason for hope anymore, but as long as I didn't hear those words, I still had reason for hope.

One of the moms, Sadie, encouraged me that the touch from a loved one can lead to the desire of wanting to work through a difficult situation. That made sense. My heart resonated with her words of encouragement. Sadie's question, "What do you have to lose, it appears you're already being rejected?" made even more sense.

Sadie was right, I had nothing to lose that I hadn't already lost.

My Bible verse that day was *"Fools think their own way is right, but the wise listen to others" (Proverbs 12:15 NLT).* It didn't resonate with me earlier in the day, but it sure did during my meeting, the one I didn't want to go to. The words "have courage and trust" finally made sense. I needed to have courage to face the truth and trust God to lead me through my circumstance to receive what He wanted me to receive. I realized God had been giving me the answer all along through advice from others when I asked Him what He wanted me to have courage for. *Who would have thought He would have gotten through to me at a PTA meeting?*

> *I waited patiently for the LORD; he inclined*
> *to me and heard my cry. (Psalm 40:1 ESV)*

POINTS TO PONDER

When you don't know what to do, do what you know to do... pray, and then listen.

Perhaps you're in a situation that is ongoing and you don't know which way to turn anymore. Perhaps you've been praying, but you've not received an answer.

Often the answer to our questions, dear one, to our prayer, is to simply be still and wait until we learn or are told what to do. Sometimes, however, God responds quickly, but because of doubt or fear, we fail to act on His response, and time stands still. Pay attention, be listening, watching, and willing to act on the Holy Spirit's promptings. It may be that the Lord is silent because He's waiting on you to take the next step.

> *Cast your cares on the LORD and he will sus-*
> *tain you; he will never let the righteous fall. (Psalm*
> *55:22 NIV)*

Prayer: Heavenly Father, thank You that You know and see everything, even the times I fail so I can be corrected. Thank You that tomorrow is a new day for a fresh start. Please forgive me for my moments of weakness when I doubt or fear, and please speak to me in a clear way that I can understand and be guided. Help me to keep hope alive in my spirit even if the journey gets long and sometimes frustrating. Help me, Jesus, to rejoice in these moments, to be still, and to keep faith that You are working everything out for the good of all. Thank You for sending the right people in my life at the right time and for those who are a constant in my life to offer encouragement and support. Help me please, to keep my eyes, ears, heart, and mind open to Your Holy Spirit's promptings and to act on them in faith. I pray this in Your holy name. Amen.

Chapter 15

―❦―

GOD RESCUES

*The LORD is close to the brokenhearted; he
rescues those whose spirits are crushed.*

—Psalm 34:18 (NLT)

Grateful for the insight of friends from PTA, I shared with Jenna the advice the moms gave about going to visit Ryan. Jenna had two words for me. "Do it!"

Wondering how to go about my visit, I recalled Ryan telling me that he missed coming home to the smell of a meal cooking after a long day at work and getting to sit down with his family. I happened to have off from school for spring break that coming Friday. Jenna offered to stay with her friend, Taryn on that day so I could cook supper for Ryan and surprise him when he walked in the door.

Feeling confident about my decision, I shared my plans with Eric, my parents, Ryan's parents, the pastor, the priest, my counselor, and my sisters. All of them were supportive of my decision and wished the best for Ryan and me.

That morning, my devotion came from *Philippians 1:6 (ESV),* *"And I am sure of this, that he who began a good work in you will bring it to completion at the day of Jesus Christ."* The devotion explained that taking the first step is not always the hardest, but continuing to trust and live by faith after that first step is taken, can be more difficult. But we are not to be discouraged even if we get knocked down, for the One who leads us to our first step will bring our journey to completion because He is faithful.

I had the opportunity to visit with my counselor on the morning of the day I planned to visit Ryan. He encouraged me with *Matthew 14:28–29 (NIV), "'Lord, if it is you,' Peter replied, 'tell me to come to you on the water,' 'Come,' he said. Then Peter got down out of the boat, walked on the water and came toward Jesus."*

My counselor shared that, like Peter, I too decided to leave my boat of security by taking a step in faith to go to Ryan. He cautioned me to remember to stay focused on my trust in Jesus and not let myself sink from the waves of the storm. For as long as Peter trusted Jesus, he was able to walk on water. But when he took his focus off Jesus and looked at the frightening waves on the water, he began to sink.

> *But when he saw the wind, he was afraid and, beginning to sink, he cried out, "Lord, save me!" Immediately Jesus reached out his hand and caught him. "You of little faith," he said, "Why did you doubt?" And when they climbed into the boat, the wind died down. (Matthew 14:30–32 NIV)*

I believed God would carry me through the storm as long as I trusted Him and kept my focus on Him rather than on my circumstance. For a reminder to help keep my focus and stay encouraged, I wore the footprints necklace that Jenna had given as a present. Every bit of encouragement helped.

I gathered my groceries and was all set for surprising Ryan. After dropping Jenna off at Taryn's house, I called my mom, my mother-in-law, and my sister, Mary, to let them know I was on my way. The closer I arrived at my destination, the more nervous I felt. I wondered what Ryan's reaction would be when he saw me. I wondered if Ryan still loved me and what we would talk about.

When I arrived at Ryan's house, I prayed for courage as I took the next step and went inside. Once inside, I got busy preparing supper and set the table for two with the tablecloth I borrowed from my mother-in-law, china from my house, flowers from the flower shop, and candles to set the mood. I chilled the wine and set a card I made for Ryan next to the flowers I bought for him.

According to his schedule, Ryan was due to be home any minute. I watched out the window and paced the floor while waiting for his arrival. An hour had passed. Worry started getting the best of me that perhaps Ryan feared coming inside after seeing my car parked outside. I calmed myself, however, with the hope that Ryan got held up at work.

Another hour passed. Ryan was now two hours late from when I expected him. By this time, I was concerned. I called his mother to tell her Ryan hadn't yet arrived home. She offered to call Ryan to see if he was still at the office.

She called back with a heavy sigh saying Ryan didn't answer the phone, which meant he was probably no longer at work and perhaps it was so that he feared coming home. I hung my head in sorrow. Even Ryan's mom feared the worst. I prayed for strength to accept that Ryan perhaps wasn't ready to see me.

Just then, however, I saw headlights pull into the driveway. I told my mother-in-law I would call her back and we said goodbye. I remained seated in the den to give Ryan the chance to gather his thoughts after realizing I was there and prepared supper for the two of us. After a moment, I got up to greet him.

A sigh of relief came over me from the smile I saw on Ryan's face. We fell into each other's arms and hugged a big hug which was long overdue. I smiled and said, "I take it you're not upset that I came."

Crying uncontrollably all the while we hugged, Ryan said, "Not at all. I'm so happy to see you."

He was delayed in coming home, he said, by an unexpected customer who needed assistance.

I thanked God for coming through… Great is His faithfulness!

Great is his faithfulness; his mercies begin afresh each morning. (Lamentations 3:23 NLT)

While Ryan cleaned up for supper, I called his mom back to inform her that Ryan arrived home and appeared happy to see me!

Rather than bringing up our circumstance, I listened instead to Ryan talk about everyday life so as not to make him feel pressured. I tried not to fix where we may have gone wrong or figure anything out. I simply appreciated the moment. I was thankful for accepting what I believed God wanted me to embrace.

Perhaps God has been faithful to come through for you as well. Or maybe you're caught in the struggle of accepting something God is asking for you to embrace.

Ryan and I parted the following day, making no promises or having expectations of promises already made. I simply thanked God for the time I had with Ryan and trusted He'd lead the way to go from there.

While on my way home, I listened to a message from Pastor Kerry Shook. "Without doubt, there's no need for faith," he said.

His words got my attention, for if we never doubt, there'd be no reason to hope for God to come through. I learned that life goes smoother if we obey, despite our doubt and fear, and hope instead that our God will be faithful. I asked God to help me stay in faith even when my circumstance was uncertain.

When I arrived home, I had a message from Ryan thanking me for having the courage it took to risk coming to see him. I was encouraged to see that the scripture my counselor shared with me the day before about Peter keeping his focus on Jesus was the same scripture in my devotion that day I arrived home. It confirmed that Jesus spoke through my counselor.

I shared, of course, with those who encouraged me to go see Ryan.

Ryan and I started seeing each other on the weekends again. Physically, Ryan was there, his heart, however, continued to seem miles away. How we got so far from where we used to be, I didn't understand. Where we were headed, I didn't know. I struggled with the distance that seemed to remain between us, yet hope still lived in my spirit that God would do a wondrous work in my marriage. I prayed Ryan and I would rekindle the love we once had.

For you are great and do wondrous things, you
alone are God. (Psalm 86:10 ESV)

The end of the school year was quickly approaching and both Ryan's daughter and Lauren were graduating. Since the graduations were on the same day, I explained to Eric and Lauren that I planned to attend my stepdaughter's graduation, but would attend Lauren's reception. Eric and Lauren understood me wanting to be there for Ryan and his daughter.

With graduation being only a day away, I shared with Ryan over the phone that I'd enjoy attending his daughter's graduation with him. I was disheartened, however, for it was my understanding that Ryan thought it would be best for him to attend the ceremony on his own. Perhaps it was more of a struggle for him than I thought that his daughter was graduating and moving away.

I didn't understand. *Ecclesiastics 4:10 (BSB)* explains *"For if one falls down, his companion can lift him up."* I wanted to be there to support Ryan as well as my stepdaughter, who invited me. It seemed though I was in the way. It seemed we repeatedly took one step forward and two steps back. I didn't know how to help Ryan. It appeared that if I pressured him, I only pushed him farther. *What else was I to do, but stay away?*

I hung up the phone with tears I couldn't control. Lauren asked what had happened. I expressed my hurt and frustration about wanting to be a support, but not feeling welcome. Lauren was sympathetic. She said she'd be happy to have me at her graduation.

As it turned out, I was honored to attend Lauren's graduation with Eric, Jenna, and Lauren's family. I would have regretted missing the event of someone special who wanted me present.

211

Jenna graduated too, from middle school that is. I was privileged to get to walk into school every day with her for three years and to get to see her and her friends in the hall daily. I was going to miss Jenna and her friends stopping by my desk throughout the day. I was thankful, however, that I still had her at home.

With school out and summer vacation beginning, I spent time at the church visiting with the priest about my circumstance. I was getting burned out fighting for my marriage, seeing no sign of it growing. Nobody had the answer to what to do next—not even the priest. I found peace, however, in his encouraging words, "You've prayed. Find comfort in knowing your prayer is in God's hands."

I was sure it was only a matter of time for God to come through like He always had.

I call on you, my God, for you will answer me;
turn your ear to my prayer. (Psalm 17:6 NIV)

Eric was home from college for the summer and interning with an agronomy company just a few miles from our community. I didn't have many weddings booked at the lodge that I managed, so Jenna and I took on the task of tree cleaning for her dad's newly planted groves of trees for the hunting business he continued to operate. We spent a couple of days a week picking rocks, cutting grass between the rows of trees, and pulling weeds around each tree. We joined my mom and dad for supper and spent an overnight with them on the days we worked on the groves of trees. Mom's homemade meals and desserts were a treat after a hard day of work. Before heading back to our house, I gave Mom and Dad's house a good cleaning to show my appreciation. It was a small act of kindness for all they had done for me.

I enjoyed having Eric home for the summer. I treasured the precious moments working alongside Jenna on the farm and our conversation on the drive to and from our hometown. Jenna shared openly about her struggle involving the divorce between her dad and me and the lessons she took away from the experience. She learned the importance of being a good listener and obeying while planning for the future. She learned to lean on God and to trust Him to come through for her. I am confident that Jenna will be an inspiration to others as they seek their calling. I am also confident that she will be a support to others going through a situation similar to hers.

Cherish every moment with those you love
at every stage of your journey. (Jack Layton)

The She Speaks Conference through the Proverbs 31 Ministry was coming up. I worked on preparing my book proposal for the book I had been writing for presentation to several agents and editors who I was scheduled to meet with.

When the week of the conference arrived, Jenna, Brad, and I flew to North Carolina for the event. Upon arriving, I realized my luggage was missing. I wasn't pleased, of course, and panicked over what I'd wear. Jenna assured me that she had plenty of clothes packed and I was welcome to any of it. She also reassured me that there must be a reason for the missing luggage.

While walking in the parking lot on our way to the hotel, I came across three pennies, which to me was a sign to trust all would be well, for it is written, "In God we trust," on coins. I am a firm believer that God miraculously places pennies in our paths, or coins, when He wants to remind us to keep our trust in Him. I was confident my luggage would appear in three days because of the three pennies I came across.

Jenna pointed out to me that I frequently come across pennies. I do! Perhaps it is because I need lots of reminding to put my trust in God!

Losing my luggage wasn't the only experience I wasn't expecting. At the very start of the conference, an elderly woman, who I never saw again, approached me in the hall and said she felt led to share that I was holding on to false hope in a relationship. I had no words to respond. My heart felt heavy from the message given. I continued though, to participate in the conference with a positive attitude after saying a prayer to God for me to be a good listener to what He would reveal.

While at the conference, I had opportunity to meet and hear from Lysa TerKeurst, Renee Swope, and numerous other Christian authors and inspirational speakers. I met several wonderful women, all desiring to write, speak, or do both. I learned a great deal of information as far as writing and speaking and was fortunate to meet with several agents and editors to view my proposal. I was disappointed, however, that none of them showed interest in my story. Instead, every one of them encouraged me that when I find healing within my marriage, my story will then be ready for completion.

Frustrated that my marriage was in the condition it was, I blamed my husband for my story not being completed. I asked God why He brought me to the conference in the first place when my story wasn't ready to be accepted.

"It's not about you" was the response that I felt in my spirit.

I didn't understand the response at the time, but was enlightened at the church service I attended the following day with Jenna and her dad. During the message, the priest pointed out that God is the receiver of all glory and not us. I realized that the lessons I learned through my struggle weren't for my benefit, but for the benefit of others so that they may be brought to Jesus and glorify Him.

> *Not to us, LORD, not to us but to your name*
> *be the glory, because of your love and faithfulness.*
> *(Psalm 115:1 NIV)*

It was for good reason that the agents and editors turned down my book proposal. God wasn't done teaching me what He wanted me to teach others. My story wasn't complete and didn't yet have the ending I believed God intended it to have to make a positive impact on the lives of others. I believed in my heart though, that an inspiring ending was on the way, lessons would be passed to others, and God would receive the glory! I was thankful for all that I took away from the conference.

> *But these things I plan won't happen right*
> *away. Slowly, steadily, surely, the time approaches*

*when the vision will be fulfilled. If it seems slow, do
not despair, for these things will surely come to pass.
Just be patient! They will not be overdue a single
day! (Habakkuk 2:3 TLB)*

While I never learned the reason why my luggage went missing, I got by just fine with the clothes that Jenna packed and just as I thought, my luggage was found on the third day, the last day of the conference. It was at the airport all along, jammed inside the conveyer system.

Surprisingly, my luggage went missing on the trip back as well, along with Jenna's luggage! The reason for our missing luggage may simply have been to test our patience and trust in God to come through. Jenna wasn't as accepting of her luggage missing as she was mine, but both our luggage was returned to us!

My marriage continued to be a struggle the remainder of the summer. I gave thought to the message given to me by the woman during the conference. To keep from getting down, I put my energy into showing appreciation for the love given by my children and family and into writing my story that I believed had a purpose.

Maybe you're going through a struggle, too, and are in need of encouragement to hold tight to what you believe.

Seeking insight and encouragement from someone dear to me, I shared with them my hope to make a positive impact on the lives of others through the story I was writing. Instead of offering support and an encouraging word, my friend expressed the lack of interest people have in reading sob stories. I could have let their opinion bother me, but I didn't. I see the story of my life as an inspiring story about growing in my faith during a difficult time, developing a relationship with our Lord, and trusting in His promises, amazing love, grace, and power! I felt all the more encouraged to share my story… God's story!

*Don't be afraid. I have rescued you. I have
called you by name; now you belong to me. (Isaiah
43:1 CEV)*

215

POINTS TO PONDER

Perhaps you feel anxious, sad, or maybe even hopeless about a circumstance in your life.

Invite God into your situation, dear one, and find comfort when you invite Him and pray in knowing that your prayer is in God's hands and that He will take care of you.

Perhaps God has come through for you in a situation... Praise God always for His faithfulness!

Let them give glory to the LORD and declare
his praise in the coastlands. (Isaiah 42:12 ESV)

Prayer: Thank You, good and sovereign Lord, for Your faithfulness. Thank You that You are my hope. Help me always to invite You into my circumstances, to leave my boat of security, and to stay in faith after taking the first step to trust You. Thank You for rescuing me through Your endless love and for providing for all my needs. Forgive me please, for the times I'm tempted to give up or lose sight of You, our almighty, all powerful God. Forgive me also for the times I've made my circumstances about me. Thank You that I don't have to rely on my own strength when circumstances get difficult. Help me to trust in You even when my circumstance seems hopeless, to be grateful for what I have, to praise You while I wait for the storm to pass, and to accept what You want me to embrace. Help me to be patient for my dream to come to pass, to never take Your love for granted, and to give You, God our Father, the glory. I pray this in Your holy name, Christ Jesus. Amen.

Chapter 16

ACCEPT

There is a time for everything, and a season for every activity under the heavens: a time to be born and a time to die, a time to plant and a time to uproot, a time to kill and a time to heal, a time to tear down and a time to build, a time to weep and a time to laugh, a time to mourn and a time to dance, a time to scatter stones and a time to gather them, a time to embrace and a time to refrain from embracing, a time to search and a time to give up, a time to keep and a time to throw away, a time to tear and a time to mend, a time to be silent and a time to speak, a time to love and a time to hate, a time for war and a time for peace.

—Ecclesiastes 3:1–8 (NIV)

As usual, summer came to an end, quicker than I wanted. Eric packed up his things to head back to college for his sophomore year and out poured my tears, just like the first year. Lauren chose the same college and headed off with him. I looked forward to their return before they even made it out of the driveway. I was confident, however, that everything was going to be okay.

I, too, was back at school as was Jenna. She was a freshman in high school and of age to drive herself to school which was five minutes from the middle school where I was. I missed going to school with her and seeing her in the halls. Before long though, I got used to the new routine and was busy attending her school activities and sports events.

When Jenna wasn't busy with school events or hanging out with her friend, Brooke, we sat in her bedroom and talked sometimes for hours. Many of those nights Jenna was treated to a back or foot rub which both she and her brother were used to from baby on. When Brooke visited, I was fortunate to get to know her and was often included in conversation between her and Jenna. I cared a great deal for Brooke's well-being like I did for my own daughter.

I treasured the closeness Jenna and I developed. Had Ryan been living with us, the bond between she and I may not have grown as strong as it did.

> Motherhood is not a hobby, it is a calling...
> It is not something to do if you can squeeze the
> time in. It is what God gave you time for. (Elder
> Neil L. Andersen)

That fall some changes took place at the lodge that I had been managing for several years. The income my position provided helped to make ends meet financially for my family and me. But after prayerfully discerning what to do when the business changed ownership, I informed Bill that I would no longer be a part of it.

Bill felt bad, for he knew how much I needed the income from a second job. While praying that I would be provided for, a thought came to his mind. He was given the idea to design a Prayer Capsule. I thought it interesting, for Bill wasn't one to think up something of that nature on his own. I believed God gave Bill the idea to design such a thing. Bill held to the belief that he indeed was prompted by the Holy Spirit. Had I not been on my own to provide for my family and me, Bill may never have prayed for God to provide for me.

Bill invited me to be his business partner. Together, we worked on the design of a capsule meant as a keepsake to hold and protect a prayer written for one's self, a loved one, or anyone in need of prayer for any particular reason. It was our intent that the Prayer Capsule would lead people to Jesus through the power of prayer.

While I enjoyed time with Jenna at home and helped design the Prayer Capsule, Eric enjoyed his experience at college. Instead of living in a dorm, he lived with his friends, known as his "brothers," in the Farmhouse Fraternity he joined the previous year. The fraternity offered their services to organizations in the community where he attended college. They held formals in the fall and spring of the year for the members and their families that Jenna, Brad, and I enjoyed attending.

As time passed, another Christmas arrived. I spent Christmas with my family and Ryan spent it with his family. By this time, I received little support to stay married. One of my closest friends, Samantha, who had a solid faith, reached out to me over the holiday and shared that the verse *"For I know the plans I have for you,' declares the LORD, 'plans to prosper you and not to harm you, plans to give you hope and a future'" (Jeremiah 29:11 NIV)* had come to her while praying about my circumstance.

Samantha shared that she was concerned, for it seemed my marriage was doing me and my children harm rather than good. I understood what Samantha was saying. I admit it had taken a toll on me… it was tiring. I didn't want to give up though. I wanted to believe that God wanted to restore my marriage and that He wanted me to stay in faith that He would come through and provide. I had such hope that Ryan would have a change of heart and fight for our marriage. I believed that all things were possible with God.

> *But with God all things are possible. (Matthew 19:26 NIV)*

Wanting to know where Eric and Jenna stood with my circumstance, I went to each of them and asked what I was teaching them by continuing to stay married. Eric said he knew I stayed married because my faith was in the Lord to come through and provide. Jenna knew my faith in the Lord was strong, but believed that I was taken advantage of because I failed to set boundaries. While Eric understood my determination to hang on, Jenna was well aware that I dug my own self in a rut because all too often I lacked setting boundaries which opened the door for me to be mistreated.

I made the decision to strive to be faithful to God's will by doing my best to preserve my marriage, but to set necessary boundaries. I took a stand and told Ryan I expected nothing less than for both he and I to make the decision to commit to our marriage. I stated also that I was no longer willing to settle for my husband to simply visit on the weekends.

Weeks passed without any change. On Valentine's Day, I received a card and present from Eric and Lauren and an invitation to join them for the hockey game in town that Friday evening. I accepted their invitation and was grateful I had them to lean on. The love my children demonstrated reminded me very much of the love demonstrated between the mother and the child in the story, *Love You Forever*, that I enjoyed reading to them when they were young.

Along came spring and another school year came to a close. I tended to the groves of trees over the summer again with Jenna for her dad, as well as fixed fence and did some work around the yard and in the house for him. Eric continued to intern with the agronomy company in the area. Keeping thousands of trees clean was none too enjoyable. It was long and tedious, but it provided time with Jenna, opportunity for communication that was an important part of our relationship, and a summer income for both of us.

Bill and I launched the Prayer Capsule that summer and marketed it to local and distant stores as well as online sites. I prayed God-sized prayers that people all over the world would be touched by giving and receiving the gift of prayer.

I used the Prayer Capsule myself by writing a prayer on the scroll inside, asking God to transform the hearts of Ryan and me into hearts for Him and to heal our broken marriage. Along with my prayer, I included a list of qualities I desired in my relationship with Ryan and a request that if it wasn't God's will for our marriage to be restored that He would bring the man He intended for me into my life. I tucked my prayer to God inside the capsule and trusted He would answer.

> *Don't burn out; keep yourselves fueled and aflame. Be alert servants of the Master, cheerfully expectant. Don't quit in hard times; pray all the harder. (Romans 12:11–12 MSG)*

Several weeks later, I ran into a friend of mine, Dan, a teacher that I worked with who coached sports. He and I had gotten to know each other through sharing Christian books with one another and discussing our thoughts on the author's viewpoints. He was a fine Christian man who taught Bible study and offered to pray if he knew somebody was struggling. Even though our visit was brief, it was timely, I thought, that I ran into Dan and had the opportunity to say hello as I had been thinking about some of the conversations he and I shared previously about facing struggles and rising above them.

Another school year started back up. Jenna started her sophomore year in high school and Eric was a junior in college already. Jenna continued participating in sports and Eric continued being a Farmhouse Member. As for me, I hadn't seen Ryan for most of the summer. Our marriage looked hopeless, but I believed in miracles and hoped for one still.

> *LORD, you know the hopes of the hopeless. Surely you will hear their cries and comfort them. (Psalm 10:17 NLT)*

With school back in session, Dan and I ran into each other regularly and visited. I shared the struggle I was going through in my marriage in which he offered to pray on the spot. "I don't know what your future holds," he encouraged, "but I do know Who holds your future."

I liked that. It gave me comfort in knowing that I didn't have to know the outcome of my circumstance, but to know my marriage was in God's hands and that in His hands it was safe.

Several months later, Dan offered to reach out to Ryan to pray with him and encourage him to work toward restoring our marriage. I had hope that Ryan would see things in a different light coming from someone other than me or the pastor, so I agreed for Dan to reach out to Ryan.

The two of them met within a couple of weeks. Dan listened to what Ryan had to share and offered a prayer in which Ryan accepted. After their conversation and the prayer Dan offered, I had hope that Ryan would have an awakening and desire for our marriage to be restored.

I never heard from Ryan. *Was he still in need of putting things in order with his life before he could focus on our marriage? Was the prayer my friend prayed not of God's will?* I wasn't sure, but I felt sad and my spirit felt weak… I wanted my son's reassurance that God would come through just like Eric knew I believed He would.

After I shared with Dan that I longed for a hug from my son and his reassurance that everything will be okay, he said my son will be married and have a wife and family to take care of someday. He asked, "What if God wants you to let go of what you've been holding on to and open your heart to something new He has in store for you?"

I didn't want to hear what Dan had to say or let go of the care and support my son so willingly offered. Other than my dad, Eric was the only man I had counted on and trusted to show me real love. I didn't want to let go of my marriage either. Letting go would have been closing the door on my dream to help make the world a better place by teaching, along with Ryan, the life he and I believed God intended His children to live.

> *When I am overwhelmed, you alone know the way I should turn. (Psalm 142:3 NLT)*

I went home to Jenna and shared the conversation between Dan and me. She interrupted and demanded, "Stop hanging on to a dream that isn't going anywhere!"

Jenna looked hurt. It appeared she lost hope in my marriage. I doubted she understood. I hung on to my desire of being happily married to Ryan because I believed God gave the desire to me. *What if God wanted me to hang on just a little longer? What faith did I have if I didn't believe God would come through for me?*

"You're hurting," Jenna cried, "and I'm hurting because you're hurting!"

I didn't know what to say. I didn't want my daughter to hurt. I didn't want to go through another divorce either. *What would people think if I divorced for a second time? I wanted to work through my marriage; didn't Jenna understand that? Couldn't others understand I was willing to be patient for God to answer my prayer? What if the answer to my prayer was right around the corner?*

I prayed, "God, please show me what to do."

> *Hear my cry, O God; attend unto my prayer.*
> *(Psalm 61:1 KJV)*

Perhaps God is trying to get through to you through a trusted friend or a loved one by asking for you to let go of something you have been clinging to.

Convinced that God would make a way where there seemed to be no way even if no one else believed, I held tight to my faith that God would come through. I went to Ryan's brother and sister-in-law and poured out my heart in hopes that they could get through to Ryan. Like Ryan's mom and dad, they too appeared to be hopeful that my marriage with Ryan would be restored. They were kind to listen and offered to pray.

Several weeks later, I drove to my mom and dad's house to bake cookies with them for Christmas. As always, they asked if I heard from Ryan.

"No," I said and covered up, as usual, reassuring them that I was happy despite my struggle.

My mom paid my cover up no attention that day. She had a look of concern in her eyes that I couldn't calm. Her voice was subtle, yet serious when she shared how she and my dad were concerned because of my circumstance. This would have been my fourth year celebrating Christmas without my husband.

"Your father and I are hurting to see you hurting," my mom shared.

I thought long and hard on my drive home that day. Silencing my hurt all along had been easy; silencing the hurt of my mom and dad was not. It broke my heart to know they were hurting. I hadn't realized until then the weight that was placed on my parents because of my struggle.

I told God straight up that I did everything I thought possible to save my marriage and keep the dream my husband and I had alive, but it appeared that Ryan lost hope and even interest in our marriage. It wasn't right that loved ones were suffering.

A thought crossed my mind that if Ryan intended to commit to his promise, he would have done so by now. It came to me that God may have wanted to save my marriage, but because He gives us free will, no one can be forced to love and care for another.

Not wanting to accept what I felt in my spirit, but also not wanting loved ones to hurt, I prayed for God to speak truth to my heart and show me the way.

John 8:32 (KJV), *"And ye shall know the truth, and the truth shall make you free,"* spoke to my heart, and a still, small whisper within my spirit to let go of trying to control what I couldn't control broke through.

Just then I recalled my conversation with Jenna a few weeks ago. I broke down crying. *How could I have neglected my daughter's plea and the truth she tried to make me see?* Once again, I caused hurt to the ones I loved the most.

Realizing it may be so that God had spoken truth through Jenna when she tried explaining that I was trapped in a relationship going nowhere, as were my dreams, and through my parents when they cautioned me about hanging on, I was left to make a choice.

I recalled advice given previously from Dan. He told me God will give us ten signs or more if that's what we need to know what God wants us to do. I believed it was time that I put an end to what caused my loved ones and me to hurt the way we had been.

I apologized to Jenna for hurting her and for being so stubborn. I thanked her for speaking what she believed was the truth, even though I refused to listen at the time she shared. I thanked both her and her brother for all the times they were my eyes and my ears when I didn't see or hear. I asked them, "Why do you keep standing by me when I continue to make mistakes?"

"Because you're Mom and we love you," they said.

My goodness, I couldn't have asked for better. I appreciated the unconditional love my children demonstrated through the storm. I realized through the difficult experience of attempting to hang on that sometimes it takes more faith to walk away than to stay.

I shared with my children that I believed God was preparing me to be strong and to walk away and that if they were in agreement, my next step would be to file for divorce. They agreed that I had given my all to my marriage and that perhaps closing the door was my next move.

> Sometimes God closes doors because it's time to move forward. He knows we won't move unless circumstances force us to. (Author Unknown)

The artist, Plumb, came out with a new song, "Lord, I'm Ready Now," in which my spirit resonated with. The artist confesses having run from God and done what they wanted to do. They express that they don't want to let God down anymore. They ask for forgiveness and commit to being ready to trust in Him.

I had gotten myself into my share of circumstances and, more often than not, ran from God when He tried to rescue me. I promised God I'd pay closer attention to His prompting and obey rather than run, hide, or try to solve the problem on my own. "Lord, I'm ready," I promised. "I'm ready to listen. I'm done running, done pretending, and done trying to fix things on my own."

> *Free me from hidden traps; I want to hide in you. (Psalm 31:4 MSG)*

I contacted my lawyer to make arrangements for a divorce. I hated to see it come to this, but after holding on three-plus years to my marriage and seeing no progress and realizing the hurt I caused to those dearest to me, I couldn't justify hanging on any longer. It was time to face reality and accept that I couldn't force my husband to do what he may not have been ready to do, even if it may have been God's will.

I was scheduled to meet with my lawyer just days before Christmas to draw up the divorce papers. Eric and Lauren were home from college for the holiday break. Knowing I'd need support, they, along with Jenna, agreed to go with me to my appointment after work that day.

On my way to work the morning of my appointment, I prayed, "God, if ever I needed a time for truth to be spoken, I need it today." I knew God saw my heart. He knew I didn't want to divorce Ryan. If it wasn't God's will for me to follow through with divorce papers, I needed to know before the end of the working day that afternoon.

I heard nothing throughout the day except, "Really…taking your children with you to the lawyer?"

The voice made me doubt that my children should join me. But just when I was about to make a phone call after work to tell them it would be okay if they didn't want to join me, I received a text from Jenna reassuring me that she was still coming with. Doubt vanished, for I knew at that moment the voice in my head had come from the enemy and not God. When I pulled into the driveway, Eric and Lauren came running out of the house and said they got back from running errands just in time to be there for me. "Thank you, Jesus," I whispered.

> *Into Your hands I commit my spirit; You have redeemed me, O LORD, God of truth. (Psalm 31:5 MEV)*

Relieved that my children were going with me, a peace came over me. I said one last prayer on the way to the lawyer's office, asking for God to give me a word so I'd know for sure that it was His will for me to take the step I was about to take.

When my lawyer walked into the room where my children and I were waiting, my heart raced with fear, for God hadn't yet given me a sign that I was making the right move. After taking his seat and greeting my children, my lawyer looked at Eric, Lauren, and Jenna in the eyes and explained that their mom has been hanging on to a marriage for over three years, which is more than most would give, and waiting with hope while given empty promises. He shared with my children that they deserve to see their mom happy, loved, and cared for instead of them being concerned about me, for they too have lives to live.

In that moment, I believed God assured me through the words so well spoken by my lawyer that I had taken the right step... Sometimes God waits until the very last moment to come through.

At the right time, I, the LORD, will make it happen. (Isaiah 60:22 NLT)

POINTS TO PONDER

Are you holding onto something and masking pain instead of letting go and allowing God to lead you to a new and perhaps better door that will put a new spirit within you?

Perhaps, like me, you struggle to set boundaries and cause hurt to yourself or even loved ones.

Perhaps you feel led to make a move, but uncertainty steps in and attempts to hold you back.

Don't let negative chatter or others talk you out of where God is leading you. Surrender your circumstance to God, my friend, and allow Him to have control over your life and guide you through whatever situation you may be facing. If it's pleasing others and setting boundaries that you struggle with, know that you risk losing ground when there are no boundaries and end up getting hurt or unintentionally hurting others.

> Your decision to obey God affects other people, and when you decide to disobey God, that also affects others. (Joyce Meyers)

Prayer: Dear good and faithful God, thank You for loving me even when I run from You and try to solve my problems on my own. Thank You, Jesus, for using friends and loved ones to get through to me when I can't see. Thank You for Your perfect timing. Please forgive me for hanging on to what's hurting me or the ones that are counting on me, and for the times I run and am stubborn to obey. Help me, please, to unmask what I've been covering, to set boundaries where boundaries need to be set, and to let go of negative chatter that causes uncertainty. Help me, Jesus, to trust my future is in Your hands even when I don't know the outcome. Please give me the faith to give You complete control and to trust that You will see me through every door You lead me to. I pray this in Your precious name. Amen.

Chapter 17

GOD PROVIDES

Now to him who is able to do immeasurably more than all we ask or imagine, according to his power that is at work within us.

—Ephesians 3:20 (NIV)

I thanked my children and Lauren for their support that day. Heaviness remained in my heart, however. I still did not want to divorce Ryan, nor hurt him. I struggled with the thought of him having to see the papers and learning of my decision to file for a divorce.

The following day, I met with my lawyer's secretary to pick up the divorce papers ready to be given to Ryan. The secretary, sensing I assumed, that I was struggling with my decision to file for divorce commented, "You're having a difficult time with this, aren't you?"

I broke down with tear filled eyes and whispered, "I still love him."

She reassured me that when we face a struggle and surrender it completely to God, only then is He able to do with our situation what He knows is best to do. I thanked both the secretary and my lawyer for their kindness and encouraging words. I left the lawyer's office entrusting my situation in God's hands.

> *"For I know the plans I have for you," declares the Lord, "plans to prosper you and not to harm you, plans to give you hope for a future." (Jeremiah 29:11 NIV)*

Christmas Day was a struggle for me. My attention was drawn again and again to the wall in my parents' dining room where my wedding photo of Ryan and me hung. I couldn't help but wonder what I did wrong as well as wonder why Ryan seemed to have lost his love for me.

Thinking I wasn't enough, I whispered, "I don't understand... I thought I looked so pretty that day...why didn't he love me?"

Not knowing my dad heard my whisper, I felt the touch of his hand on my shoulder and heard what every daughter longs to hear from her dad, "You were pretty then and you're pretty now."

I rested my head on my dad's shoulder and let the words he spoke sink into my spirit.

My mom was bothered. She knew my heart was broken and that she couldn't take away my pain. "I know this hurts you," she said as she offered me a hug, "but I also know everything's going to be okay."

As a parent, I know how much it hurts to see your child hurting. I loved my mom and dad dearly and embraced the support they offered. I was done covering the hurt my heart had been carrying. I cried in my mom's arms and admitted it hurt very much... I wondered what was to come from another failed marriage. Whatever it would be, I was certain God would use my circumstance for His purpose and for my calling. The pain I suffered would not go wasted.

> If you're brave enough to say goodbye, life will reward you with a new hello. (Paulo Coehlo)

Having no reason to prolong what I believed needed to occur, I contacted Ryan at the New Year to tell him I filed for divorce. I had hoped that Ryan would fight to stay married after receiving that news. I longed for a phone call, a knock at my door…anything to prove that he loved me and didn't want to lose me. I heard no response.

Jenna was able to relate to my hurt. She and her boyfriend were going through a breakup as well. She shared that she had a better understanding of how I felt and why I hung on the way I did. Our circumstance drew us even closer to one another. We leaned on each other for support and learned a few things about love. Love isn't necessarily blissful with constant butterflies. It's meant to enhance rather than ruin, build up instead of tear down, and not to be taken for granted.

> A real man never stops trying to show a woman how much she means to him, even after he's got her. (Anonymous)

Several months passed with no sign for hope that my marriage would be restored. It appeared that Ryan was in agreement of divorce.

The court date was set for my divorce in the spring of the year, early in the morning just days before my birthday. I requested the morning off from work. I had good intentions to hold myself together and get through what needed to be done without being any more of a burden to anyone than I may have already been; my plan was to make it to work by the afternoon. Fortunately, I had the support of my friends in the office from work so if my plans didn't go accordingly, it would be understood. They had shown compassion and concern from the very start of my struggle.

While getting myself ready for the procedure, my mom called to confirm the time of court. Not wanting to burden her and my dad for the few minutes that it would take in court, I reassured my mom that I would be okay doing this last part on my own since it would be so brief. "Absolutely not," was her response, "we will be there and so will your sister."

I knew my mom and dad wouldn't take no for an answer; I had to admit, I appreciated their support of wanting to be there for me. Feeling a wreck to take this last step, I hurried to get myself dressed and make my way to the courthouse.

My parents and my sister, Mary, and her husband were already there by the time I arrived. Seeing them all made me realize what was about to happen and that I needed support more than I thought. Each of them hugged me letting me know they were there for whatever I'd need.

My lawyer then approached the waiting area. My emotions and nerves started getting the best of me, for in just a moment Ryan and I would no longer be. The dream I dreamt with him would be no more.

Oh, how I wished he'd come running up the stairs and yell, "Wait! I love you!"

"You ready for this?" my lawyer asked. I wasn't, but I knew it had to be done in order to move on.

Father, if you are willing, take this cup from me; yet not my will, but yours be done. (Luke 22:42 NIV)

While entering the courtroom, tears welled on the inside and ran down my face as I took the stand still hoping Ryan would burst forth and put an end to all of this. Looking to my parents, who were in tears because I was in tears, I prayed for strength just to get through the next few moments and for comfort for my parents who I knew were hurting.

Within a matter of minutes, the process was complete. I followed my parents, my sister, and her husband out the door in a state of disarray. My lawyer wished me well and commented to my dad that my mind was sorting through lots of thoughts at the time… It sure was.

My mom and Mary gave me a big hug. I was grateful for their support. God knew I would need them.

> *For your Father knows what you need before*
> *you ask him. (Matthew 6:8 NIV)*

My dad held me long in his arms. I sobbed and just let him hold me. "This needed to be over," he said.

I knew he meant well and may have been right, but I was still confused as to what happened to the love I believed I found. I cried, "I didn't get married to get my heart broken and go through a divorce."

> One of the hardest things to do in life, is
> letting go of what you thought was real. (Author
> Unknown)

I didn't go into work that day like I planned. The school principal, Ms. Atkins, told me ahead of time to take the day off, for I'd need that time more than I thought I would. The two secretaries, Rhonda and Dawn, that I worked with in the office extended heartfelt words letting me know they were thinking of me and suggested as well that I take the entire day off. They were friends I could count on if ever I needed a listening ear or a prayer. Rebecca, who set me up with Ryan had recently relocated to a new community, but kept in contact as well and offered support.

I took my mom and dad up on their invitation to lunch that day to celebrate my birthday and the courage the Lord provided me with. By this time, I had calmed down some and was in a more positive frame of mind. My parents' support surely was appreciated.

By the time Jenna arrived home from school and track practice, I had the opportunity to sort through my feelings and to reflect on the process of letting go. The journey had been long, but just as beauty comes from a butterfly's struggle to push its way through a tiny opening in the cocoon, I also grew beautifully because of the journey and other circumstances I didn't enjoy going through. I grew into a stronger person and developed a personal relationship with our

Lord as He continued to reveal Himself every step of the way during both good and difficult moments. My trust in Him grew solid. Had I not gone through the struggles that I did, I may have missed opportunity to witness God's faithfulness. My faith would have continued lacking what God intended it to be and I wouldn't be equipped to teach what He intends me to teach or be prepared for what was to come next.

I developed an even stronger bond with both my son and my daughter, as well as with my mom and dad. Because of the journey, I didn't have to wonder how my children would respond in a crisis. I witnessed a love so true, so faithful, and so sincere: a blessing any mom would want. I believed God had great plans for my family and me. I believed with all my heart that God would continue to provide just as He has in even the smallest of requests for my children and me.

> *We also rejoice in our sufferings, because we know that suffering produces perseverance; perseverance, character; and character, hope. (Romans 5:3–4 NIV)*

When Eric and Lauren arrived home for the weekend, they, along with Jenna, celebrated my birthday with me and a new beginning. How timely, for it was the spring of the year when so much of God's creation bursts forth with new growth.

Shortly after the celebration of a new beginning, I helped Jenna prepare for prom with a pleasant young man she had become friends with. She looked stunning in her black dress with an elegant hair style to go with it. It was an event I was happy to celebrate and grateful to help plan.

I was ready to move on with my life!

After feeling more settled with the reality of my divorce, I emailed Ryan to say a final "goodbye" and to wish him well. He replied with a sincere apology that helped put closure on what I had hoped for us. He expressed that he hadn't healed completely from the experience of his divorce prior to meeting me, or from the limited time he had with his daughters. Truthfully, I sensed this while we were dating and should have listened to that still, small voice within instead of believing my love for him would have been the healing he needed to start anew. I forgave Ryan, truly I did. It was necessary for the sake of my relationship with our Lord. I believed Ryan truly did love me like he said he did, that he truly wished for our dreams to come true as husband and wife, and that with the proper healing, our story may not have ended the way it did. My love for him remained. I believed in my heart, however, that I made the decision that will lead my loved ones and me down a brighter and better path. My prayers for this kind and gentle man who I had fallen in love with will remain.

Toward the end of the school year, the after-school program at the church with the pastor who counseled me while I was married, needed a teacher's aide. The pastor invited me to consider applying for the job, in which I did, and was offered the position for a couple of hours every day after school. It was an enjoyable way to earn a needed extra income.

After the school year ended, Jenna and I cleaned trees once again during the summer for her dad. We spent our overnight with my mom and dad as usual and I continued to clean their house for them. As always, Mom's cooking and her and Dad's company after a hard day in the field was a treat to come home to. That, and conversation between my daughter and me during the drive, were the best parts of the summer job!

One of the conversations between Jenna and me involved an embarrassing moment of mine, but attached with a valuable lesson. I got quite the sunburn the first day we cleaned trees and my daughter inquired whether I used sunscreen. "I did," I responded.

My face got sunburned again the following week. And again, Jenna inquired, "Are you using sunscreen?"

I assured her that I was. The third time we were about to leave the house for another day of tree cleaning, a whisper within stated, "You put hair conditioner on your face."

I was quite sure I didn't. I continued walking out the door and the whisper persisted, "That's why you got sunburned."

Since I promised God I'd pay closer attention and obey at the sound of His prompting, I put my glasses on to take a closer look at the product I used on my face and realized I did indeed put hair conditioner on my face! I had received a sample of face and hair products in the mail, one of them being sunscreen. Without taking a moment to put my glasses on the first time I used the product, I grabbed what I thought was sunscreen and put it on my face, not once, not twice, but three times.

Because the mystery was solved as to why I got sunburned two weeks in a row, I shared with Jenna what happened. The experience gave both of us a good laugh, however, I advised Jenna not to dismiss what she may think is just a silly thought passing through her mind. For all too often, we overlook God's promptings and make life more troublesome for ourselves. What is true is that God cares even about the small matters of life, even sunburns! The more readily we are willing to listen, the easier it becomes to recognize our Shepherd's voice.

My sheep hear my voice, and I know them,
and they follow me. (John 10:27 KJV)

Eric helped on his dad's farm, too, that summer. He did fencing that Jenna and I helped with. Fencing wasn't my favorite farm chore, but if it meant spending time with my children, I was up for it.

I started doing a Bible study with Dan. Dan was wise in understanding scripture from the Bible. We met once a week to go through our study and to share how we could relate what we learned to the experiences we had or were currently experiencing. We ended each session with laying hands on each other in prayer, which we were both used to when growing up.

When school started back up, Jenna was a junior in high school and Eric was on his fourth year of college. Dan invited me to pick apples with him that fall. Apple picking turned into an invitation for apple juicing and apple slicing with him. Apple slicing turned into apple baking.

After returning home from Bible study one evening, Jenna asked, "Do you like him?" referring to Dan, who she knew as a teacher and coach.

I responded, "Yes, for a friend," and explained that I wasn't looking for a serious relationship at the time. I had still been healing from the divorce and a shattered dream only months earlier even though it had been over a year since I last saw Ryan. After Jenna asked several more times if I liked Dan, I questioned, "Why do you ask?"

She explained that she wondered because my spirit seemed alive after returning home from Bible study. Without realizing the liveliness in my spirit that Jenna recognized, I simply responded, "Well, of course! It's Bible study and studying the Bible is inspiring!"

Jenna's insight reminded me of my prayer request to God for a relationship with qualities I was looking for with a companion. I was prompted to take out the scroll from the Prayer Capsule. I read through the list of qualities and realized my relationship with Dan is what I had been looking for.

> *And whatever you ask in prayer, you will*
> *receive, if you have faith. (Matthew 21:22 ESV)*

I went back into Jenna's bedroom with the list of qualities in my hand, jumped up on her bed, and said, "Look! This is my prayer I wrote a while back!"

After explaining to Jenna that God answered my prayer, she smiled as though she already knew. Jenna could relate, for she too was seeing someone who put a spark in her disposition that made her smile. Perhaps it was safe to open my heart to someone God may have sent to pick me up from the ground and love me.

> A bitter woman says, "All men are the same."
> A wise woman decides to stop choosing the same
> type of men. (Crytalina Evert)

I cherished the relationship Jenna and I had and our talks. She picked me up when I was down. I picked her up when she was down.

She spoke truth when I didn't see it. I spoke it when she needed it. She encouraged me to believe all things are possible as I did for her. She was wise for her age and was my inspiration to take hold of my dreams and not let go. If she witnessed me living my dreams, I was confident she would be inspired to live hers.

> *A sweet friendship refreshes the soul. (Proverbs 27:9)*

Jenna had come such a long way from when her brother was still in high school. I truly was blessed to still have her home with me like she had reassured me when Eric left for college. I hadn't realized at the time the relationship and blessing that would develop from her and I having this time together and that we'd be the support and inspiration for each other that we had become. The relationship with my daughter compared to a relationship with a best friend.

> *And I will give you a new heart, and I will put a new spirit in you. I will take out your stony, stubborn heart and give you a tender, responsive heart. (Ezekiel 36:26 NLT)*

Eric had known about Dan and me meeting for Bible study and hanging out while picking and processing apples. From what Eric learned about Dan from Jenna and me, it seemed he thought Dan was a nice guy. After realizing that God may have sent him to me for more than just a friend, Eric was curious about meeting Dan and seeing for himself with whom I was spending my time.

We invited Dan for Thanksgiving to our house. Eric and Dan learned they have a lot in common, hunting being one of them. After carrying on with conversation throughout the night, Eric shared that Dan came across to him as solid, confident, and pleasant to visit with. All in all, Eric seemed to like Dan.

Dan and I continued doing activities together from Bible study to picking apples to dancing in the kitchen while listening to music from the sixties. My mom and dad had been eager to meet Dan as well. They met him at my house when he was cleaning up our mess from processing apples and washing the dishes. Right then and there my dad expressed that he liked what he saw.

Dan wooed my parents with his fun-loving character and genuine personality. He was the kind of guy who was just what you see—just a hard-working, good, honest, Christian man. My mom and dad and both of my children saw that in him.

The following summer Jenna and I took a break from the farm work for her dad. Instead, I helped with the summer school program through the school system in the special needs classroom. Jenna took a job in town with a daycare program. Eric continued to intern with the agronomy company he had been with during college.

I took advantage of helping Jenna prepare that summer for her upcoming senior and final year at high school. I joined her for her senior pictures which I enjoyed. It brought back memories of being involved in Eric's senior pictures only five years prior.

I toured colleges with Jenna as well that summer. Our community had two colleges that offered a great education, but Jenna wanted the experience of attending college outside of her community. I understood that. Most of the colleges we toured were two hours from home. Lauren joined us for one of the tours. That was a fun girls' day. I liked the three of us hanging out. I liked us sharing girl talk and hoped we'd all stay close as I was quite certain Lauren was going to one day be my daughter-in-law.

The college Jenna picked was the same as her brother and Lauren's choice, a couple of hours from the community where we lived. Brooke picked that one as well, so it was reassuring to know the girls would have each other to count on while away at college and that Jenna would be close to home.

Dan joined me for visits with my mom and dad. I liked that he showed an appreciation for my parents. My parents were happy that he was in my life. I could tell my dad was at peace with where he saw my life was headed with Dan. In fact, I hadn't seen my dad that happy in years. It used to be he was concerned about me because of my previous experiences. He teased Dan and me that he liked our visits because he got out of doing dishes because we did them. Dad had a great sense of humor and a sharp mind.

Dan and I visited his parents as well. The visits weren't as frequent since they lived farther away, but I surely felt welcomed and I enjoyed the time we had together. I noticed that Dan's dad is a lot like Dan, jovial and a true hunter at heart. His mom reminded me of my mom and me, tidy and a good cook who never sits still. I liked Dan's parents the very first time I met them. They appeared to be fine Christians such as Dan. It was easy for me to see why Dan is the man he is. I was pleased with the direction my life was taking.

During that summer, Dan asked my mom, my dad, Eric, and Jenna for permission to have my hand in marriage. They all seemed happy to say, "Yes." They were fond of Dan who had fallen in love with the woman they all cared for and loved. My heart fell in love with Dan's soul and his heart that I believed to be true to his word and honorable.

His request must have given my children, as well as my mom and dad, a peace of mind believing a good man came along to love and care for their mom and their daughter.

After being given permission to marry me, Dan got down on his knee and proposed to me at an outdoor event at a winery where we were enjoying a folk concert. It was a beautiful summer evening with a crowd of people and my friend, Rebecca, and her husband present. I said yes, for I believed God sent this man to love, cherish, and adore me and for me to love, honor, and respect.

I was pleased to learn that Dan asked for my parents' and children's permission to marry me. It showed that he honored and respected not only me, but also those he knew were dearest to me.

He shared with his mom and dad and his son and daughter as well, who were close in age to my children, that he planned to propose to me. I appreciated Dan's family. His parents and children were good-hearted, like he was. His children were kind to express their thankfulness for me coming into their dad's life. That meant so very much to me that they were grateful. His family is a solid, Christian family respected and liked by many.

Friends and family were pleased to hear the news of Dan and me.

> *He lifted me out of the pit of despair, out of the mud and the mire. He set my feet on solid ground and steadied me as I walked along. (Psalm 40:2 NLT)*

POINTS TO PONDER

Perhaps you're struggling with a circumstance that you know is the right thing to do, but it's breaking your heart to have to face it.

Perhaps you also struggle with accepting help from others.

May I remind you, dear one, to invite God into your circumstance and trust that when you surrender it completely to our Lord, He will do what He knows is best with it. He will also provide you with friends and loved ones during times of need. It is His gift to you.

> *Praise be to God, who has not rejected my prayer or withheld his love from me! (Psalm 66:20 NIV)*

Prayer: Heavenly Father, thank You that You know what I need even before I ask and that You provide. Help me to pay attention to even the smallest promptings You place upon my heart. Help me to come to You and ask for my needs even when You are aware of them as this builds a more personal relationship with You. Forgive me, please, for the times I have failed to surrender my everything to You, and instead, leaned on my own strength for what may have seemed even a small task. Thank You, Jesus, for growing me through the struggles I go through and allowing me to come out even stronger and wiser. Thank You for blessing not only me because of the storm, but those dear to me. Help me, please, to trust that no matter how painful the storm I walk through, You will grow me into the person You want me to be and pour blessings forth on my life. I pray all of this in Your most holy name. Amen.

Chapter 18

—⁂—

BELIEVE

And whatever you ask in prayer, you will receive, if you have faith.

—Matthew 21:22 (ESV)

When school started back up that fall, Jenna was a senior in high school and Eric was on his last semester of college. Dan and I enjoyed sharing the news with coworkers at school that we were engaged and planning a summer wedding. We were wished well by staff as most of them knew both of us for several years and saw us as a good fit for each other.

My son proposed to Lauren, his high school sweetheart, as well. It was while they were duck hunting that Eric got down on his knee and asked Lauren to marry him. He too asked for permission for Lauren's hand in marriage from her mom and dad. We all knew the day would come when he would propose, but it was still a respectable gesture for Eric to ask for permission and not take for granted the approval of his soon to be in-laws. I was proud of Eric for being mindful of showing respect and consideration to Lauren's mom and dad.

I was happy for Eric and Lauren. I felt honored to be gaining another daughter and honored that I witnessed her and Eric's love grow over the years. For me it was a privilege...a gift I was given to enjoy. They too set their wedding date for the following summer which meant there was much to plan between Jenna's high school graduation, Eric's college graduation, and two weddings; mine, and Eric's.

Eric and Lauren and Dan and I weren't the only happy couples planning a wedding. Brad was planning a wedding as well with a wonderful woman from back home that he had fallen in love with about the time that Dan and I were getting to know each other. My children were happy for their dad as was I. It had been a prayer of mine that my children's dad finds love as well.

Eric completed his college education and graduated in early December. He waited to hear from the company he interned with during college for a job. It didn't take long for him and Lauren to both be offered a job near our hometown. Eric was hired through the agronomy company that he had been interning with. Lauren was hired through an education program in the same area.

Eric and Lauren found a home just a couple of blocks from the house that Eric, Jenna, and I lived in several years back. Meanwhile, Jenna's last track season was approaching as were her final three months of her high school education. It was her final high school prom also that she would be attending that I took pleasure in helping with.

I enjoyed the track season that year more than any other—for two reasons I suppose: I appreciated the opportunity of one final season, and I wanted Jenna to meet her goal. It was Jenna's goal every season to place at the state track meet that she had been fortunate to be a participant in during the years of her track career. This was her final year to prove herself.

Eric started packing his belongings to prepare for his move. As he created space while packing, Dan filled the space by moving some of his things into my home.

By this time, Jenna's graduation was less than a month away. It was an exciting time for her as she was graduating and planning for college. It was exciting for Eric to be starting a career, preparing for his first home, and getting married, and it was exciting for me to be getting married in just a couple of months. I believed, without a doubt, that the man I was marrying was a man of his word. God willing, there wasn't anything he wouldn't have done for me, for our relationship, and for our loved ones. I was certain of Dan's loyalty because he didn't just promise it; he proved it through his actions.

Though it was a time of joy and new beginnings for my son, my daughter, and me, I was in no way ready to let go of my children. I doubt the time would ever have come that I would have been ready. Loving my children was the most enjoyable experience I had ever had. I put my heart and soul into loving them. It was the biggest reward I had ever been given, for there was such joy in loving and serving my family and being loved in return. I clung ever so tightly to what I had with them and to the comfort of their presence. Letting go was more than "not easy." It was a heartbreaking act of love I found so very, very difficult, though necessary to do.

I prayed for strength to let go, to support my children with their dreams, and to let them spread their wings.

Perhaps you too are entering a new chapter in your life and find it difficult to let go.

> Surrender to what is. Let go of what was.
> Have faith in what will be. (Sonia Ricotti)

I took what opportunity I had of spending time with Jenna during that last year of her high school before her college education began. I treasured our late-night conversations, prayer time she requested, and foot and back rubs. I enjoyed running errands with her throughout the day, shopping together, and talking about our goals, our dreams, and just stuff. We had grown so close to each other that the thought of her being away brought such sadness to my heart. I was reminded of how difficult it was when her brother left for college and how I feared he and I would drift apart. Now I feared drifting from my daughter, this little girl of mine who had grown into a woman, a godly woman wise in her early years who I counted on for inspiration. She had become my best friend who knew just what to do and say to encourage me in the direction needed in order for me to stay on the path to my calling.

Like me, Jenna had big dreams. Her idea of living the good life was to experience life in the city along the coast with choices and options galore like I dreamed. She shared with me how she couldn't wait to see what was out there waiting for her, just like I used to share with my mom. I understood now the unease my mom must have felt when I shared my goals and when I went off to college as she too longed for continued closeness with her children. I also understood the dreams in my daughter's heart.

Jenna knew I was concerned about losing what we had, so like Eric, she too reassured me that she will always love me and that we will always be close. For my birthday that spring, she gave me a key chain with a heart that said "always" on it, another heart with the letter "J" for her name, and another heart with the words "I love you" on it to remind me of her promise.

Her present touched my heart deeply as did her heartfelt words that she shared in her card expressing how much I meant to her and how much it meant to her that she and I had the last few years, just the two of us, at home. I wanted to be close in heart forever like she promised, but close in distance too. If only I had Jenna's reassurance that she, like Eric, was going to be back when college was complete and remain in the area.

> *Be still, and know that I am God. (Psalm 46:10 NIV)*

For Mother's Day, Jenna touched my heart again. She bought us matching rings with the words "you are my sunshine" printed on them. Again, she expressed beautiful words of her love for me in a card. She shared that she chose those words for matching rings for us because we are sunshine to each other and she recalled me singing the song, "You Are My Sunshine," to her when she was little. That was a song I often heard my dad sing to my mom… I loved when Eric and Jenna expressed their love, feelings, and appreciation to me.

> *I will give thanks to you, LORD, with all my heart. I will tell of all your wonderful deeds. (Psalm 9:1 NIV)*

School wasn't quite out yet when Eric and Lauren packed up the rest of Eric's belongings. I had taken the day off to join them to meet with the caterer they chose for their wedding as well as to help pack. After the last of Eric's belongings was loaded, I fought back tears as best I could and hugged them goodbye. I had the worst sinking feeling in my heart as though I was losing them to a far-away place. They'd only be an hour away, but as I stated earlier, I didn't do well with "goodbyes" and letting go. I knew I'd miss them terribly. I'd miss them helping me cook and bake like they often did and just hanging out at the house talking with them. I'd miss hugs from my son and greeting him throughout the day.

Perhaps you can relate to the hurt in my heart if you struggle with "goodbyes" as well.

I prayed to God that my children and I would always remain close with one another like the way I believed we would when my children were young and under my wings. I prayed also for strength.

> *He gives strength to the weary and increases the power of the weak. (Isaiah 40:29 NIV)*

From there, Jenna and I made the rest of the graduation plans for her reception. We planned a joint reception with Brooke, which was really quite nice to work as a team. I enjoyed shopping with Jenna for decorations and going through photos to put on her collage. It was a bit more planning and decorating for her than it was for Eric's high school graduation…a girl thing, I suppose!

I could hardly believe that Jenna was graduating from high school already and that Eric was of age to get married, to have his own home, and to be planning a career…time had passed so quickly… much quicker than I wanted it to pass.

Jenna's reception was on the Friday evening before the Sunday graduation ceremony. It was an enjoyable occasion with family and friends who I enjoyed visiting with. The following day, Dan and I, along with Jenna, attended several of her friends' receptions together. I enjoyed making that memory with her.

On Sunday, Eric and Lauren attended the graduation ceremony with Dan and me. It was nice to have Jenna's reception early as it made graduation day less stressful and a more enjoyable time with my family.

The following week after graduation, the final track meet was yet to come. It was Jenna's last state track meet she would attend, the one she hoped to place in her favorite event, the triple jump. It was down to the last flight and Jenna waited anxiously to see if she made the finals. She did, and on her very last jump in the finals, she placed at the state track meet like she and I prayed she would! What a way to end her track and field career! She was happy! Her coaches were happy for her! I was happy for her!

I was proud of Jenna to see her accomplish her goal and stand on the podium! God is good!

This is the day the LORD has made; we will
rejoice and be glad in it. (Psalm 118:24 NLT)

Three weeks after the state track meet, my wedding day arrived…my third wedding. The thought came to me the day before my wedding that this marriage too will fail, for I am picky and too set in my ways. I hadn't expected my first marriage to end in divorce. My second failed marriage came to me as an even bigger shock. Like the Samaritan woman in *John 4:1–26 (NIV)* who had five husbands may have felt, I too carried shame in my heart.

Fearing the possibility of another failed marriage and worried that I was already looked down upon for having divorced, not one, but two husbands, and marrying for the third time, I called on God for assurance that I was making the right decision. I took to heart

God's Word, *"Therefore what God has joined together, let no one separate" (Mark 10:9 NIV).*

I then received a phone call, out of the blue, from my sister, Mary, who helped get me through my first divorce, to wish me blessings on the occasion about to take place in my life. "Funny you should call," I said, "thoughts of fear that this marriage will also fail are on my mind."

If you beat yourself up like I did and carry unnecessary shame, you know the weight from the load I'm describing.

Mary reassured me that Dan is a Godly man, a prayer answered. She encouraged me to trust that my marriage will be blessed.

My spirits were lifted after talking to Mary; I believed God used her as a vessel for Him to speak through. Instead of looking at myself as a failure and fearing that's all I'd be, I chose to believe that the love Christ showed to the Samaritan woman was mine to embrace as well. I gave my shame to the Lord and rejoiced in His love, forgiveness, and promise to work all things for the good of my family and me, as well as Dan's family and him. I went about the rest of my day preparing for my wedding and feeling confident that I was making the right decision by getting married.

Therefore, there is now no condemnation for
those who are in Christ Jesus. (Romans 8:1 NIV)

No longer feeling shame, I was excited when my wedding day arrived. Dan and I kept our ceremony simple and sentimental with just our children, who we chose as our witnesses, their significant other, and our parents.

I wore a simple, yet beautiful wedding gown that Jenna selected for me from the bridal shop in town. It was a white and elegant fitted halter dress covered with embroidered lace. Dan and our sons wore a dress shirt with a tie and our daughters wore a simple sundress. All looked exquisite, I must say.

Eric and Jenna walked me down the aisle to give me to the man God brought into our lives, while the pastor played his guitar and sang "Love Never Fails" by Brandon Heath. I was honored to have my son and daughter escort me to the altar and thankful that our loved ones joined us, including my sister, Kate, and my godchild, Rylee, who surprised us.

Following the ceremony, a reception was held for extended family and friends. It was a joyous occasion to celebrate! I was confident that God's blessings were upon my marriage and that what I found was indeed love that wouldn't fail.

A cord of three strands is not quickly broken.
(Ecclesiastes 4:12 AMP)

Adjusting to married life with Dan at my side and willing to help with chores was a big change…a good one! Because Dan helped with cooking, cleaning, gardening, canning, and laundry, my mom teased me, "Do you do anything anymore?"

My answer was, "Not as much as I used to do, but yes, Mom."

God blessed my marriage indeed! I had been given a good husband, a husband that I loved and a husband that loved in return. It felt good to be loved. My parents and my children looked happy to see me happy.

Every good and perfect gift is from above, com-
ing down from the Father of heavenly lights, who
does not change like shifting shadows. (James 1:17
NIV)

Though I woke to a new sunrise and was happy after having been given a wonderful husband, my heart was heavy for what was on the way. Two months from my wedding day, the day after my son's wedding, my daughter was scheduled to leave for college.

Prior to that day arriving, Jenna and I helped Eric and Lauren with some odds and ends in their home. Since I no longer worked a summer job, time allowed for me to make frequent trips to their house as well as to my parents' home. I enjoyed helping Eric and Lauren. I enjoyed also what time I had with Jenna before college started. She and I shopped for college necessities and I joined her for her college orientation, where we met up with her roommate, Lacy, who appeared to be a good fit for Jenna's character and personality.

Two days before Eric's wedding, Jenna and I drove to the college to move her belongings into the dorm. It was an enjoyable day organizing her dorm and just spending time together. After arriving home, Dan and I were fortunate to get to spend the evening with Eric and Lauren at the county fair in town where we checked out all the venues and toured campers, four-wheelers, and houses that were available to view.

The following day, the day before my son's wedding, I was blessed to get to spend time with him. Dan was kind enough to prepare the rehearsal supper that he and I offered to do, so I could enjoy being with Eric. While together, Eric asked if I wanted to hear the song he chose for our dance as mother and son on his wedding night. Of course, I did. Eric was always good about showing his love and appreciation for me. I wanted to hear what his heart wanted to share.

The song he chose was "Simple Man" by Shinedown. The moment I heard the lyrics, tears filled up my eyes, for the song was about an only son sharing his mother's words of advice given to him when he was young. Eric knew very well how sentimental, sensitive, and emotional I was. He looked at me, saw me crying, and got teared up himself.

I hugged Eric after the song was finished, thanked him, and told him how touched I was by his thoughtfulness. He had grown into an incredibly kind and wonderful man. I loved, appreciated, and admired everything about him. I missed him not living at home something awful, but I had much to be thankful for. For one, I was thankful for the time I had with him that day. I hoped there would always be days like that one.

After that sentimental moment with him, Jenna and I met for lunch with Lauren, her mom, grandma, and the rest of the bridesmaids. Jenna and I helped Dan finish what was left to prepare for the rehearsal supper before we headed to the church for rehearsal. I was appreciative of all the work Dan did. He's a good-hearted man, willing to do more than one would expect.

The day of the wedding went very nicely. My son looked handsome! "How did you grow up so fast on me?" I asked him. His bride was beautiful!

My mind was focused on the present for the most part, instead of what was to come in the morning; my daughter's departure.

The wedding dance kicked off with the bridal party making an entertaining entrance. From there, Eric and his lovely bride danced to a special song of theirs, followed by a song that Lauren chose to dance in the arms of her dad. The DJ then announced for me to join my son on the floor for our song, the song that Eric played for me the previous day.

I couldn't help but bury my head in the shoulders of my son and cry while I thanked God for that fine man who loved and cared for his sister and me with all his heart. I wasn't the only one who shed a tear. Eric, sentimental as well, also shed a tear. I lifted my head, smiled, and reminisced with him about some of the memories that came to my mind.

The DJ handed me the microphone after our dance. I thanked Eric and expressed that I felt like the luckiest mom to be loved by him and his sister. I thanked him for the beautiful love and care he gave to us and said to his bride, "You're a lucky lady." I meant it. My son is a wonderful man and I'm indeed a blessed mom. We gave each other a hug and got on with the dance.

My dad, knowing how difficult it was for me to let go, teared up and complimented, "That was a nice speech." And then with a sympathetic heart said, "Tomorrow you'll have to say goodbye to the other one," meaning to my daughter. The older my dad got, the more sensitive he grew. I liked that about him... I admire that in a man.

I tried not to think about having to say goodbye the next day. Thank goodness I had Dan to lean on. Had he not come into my life when he did, I'm not sure how I would have gotten through what I had to face. God is good. He is timely.

But seek first his kingdom and his righteous-
ness, and all these things will be given to you as well.

251

> *Therefore do not worry about tomorrow, for tomor-*
> *row will worry about itself. (Matthew 6:33–34*
> *NIV)*

Later during the dance, my son brought my mom and dad to the dance floor to join other couples for a special dance he and his wife planned for the couple married the most years. All the married couples at the celebration were asked to take the dance floor and one by one, those married less than sixty-four years were asked to leave the floor until only my mom and dad were left dancing. What a beautiful blessing. Mom and Dad looked so adorable and so honored to be recognized for their love for each other and their ability to still be dancing in each other's arms. The newly married couple presented the longest married couple with a gift…how sweet.

> Love is sweet when it's new, but it is sweeter
> when it's true. (Author Unknown)

The next day arrived. I felt sick to my stomach. Jenna was packed and ready to go. She said goodbye to my mom and dad who had spent the night at our house after the wedding. Dan and I walked her to the driveway. I told her to tell Dan goodbye first. He hugged her and said, "I love you… I'll take good care of your mom."

The moment Dan said he'd take good care of me, Jenna burst into a sob of tears. She and I were both crying before she reached my arms. We hugged a long hug, both crying and hanging tightly to each other. After saying, "I love you so much and will miss you," I let go and fell into my husband's arms weeping as Jenna pulled out of the driveway; letting go felt unbearable. Dan held me while I cried, but there wasn't anything he could say to take the hurt away. He knew that grieving was part of the process for me to let go.

I made my way back inside the house. My mom followed me into my bedroom and took me into her arms and held me. I cried harder yet. My mom was always good about offering compassion and her love when one of her children or grandchildren was hurting. I was grateful for my mom's compassionate love. I love her dearly. She

252

knew I was hurting and she knew just how I felt. She went through the experience ten times with my siblings and me. My dad cried too and hugged me long and hard. "I know how it hurts," he said, "I had to say goodbye too."

> How lucky am I to have something that makes saying goodbye so hard. (Winnie the Pooh)

From there, I got ready for the Sunday church service and attended it with Dan and my parents. I couldn't keep from crying during the service. I missed Jenna already. After the service, we joined Eric and his wife at the hotel for gift opening. I didn't want them to know how much I struggled to say goodbye. It was their special time and I didn't want to concern them with my struggle and put a damper on their spirits. I kept my chin up.

After helping them pack up their gifts, we headed back to the church. A special anniversary service was planned with the bishop for my parents and other couples who had been married fifty-plus years. That was quite an honor. My mom and dad celebrated their sixty-fifth wedding anniversary. I asked them what the secret was to stay married so long. They shared that they are kind with understanding, and they pray a lot together. This is good advice not only for a happy marriage, but for healthy relationships between children and parents as well.

> *Be completely humble and gentle; be patient, bearing with one another in love. (Ephesians 4:2–3 NIV)*

Had I known I would have still had both of my parents in my life at the age they were, I wouldn't have worried myself sick as a young girl over losing them. My parents were wonderful role models for my siblings and me as well as to their grandchildren and those who knew them.

When the celebration was over, we said our goodbyes to my mom and dad and family and headed back to our house as well.

The house was quiet. I struggled with the silence and the absence of Jenna. I walked past her bedroom and felt an emptiness in my heart. I couldn't see at the time how I'd get past the fact that my son and daughter had grown up and left home. I thrived on caring for them and being needed for the past twenty-four years. Letting go of the two I cared for and counted on most to hold me together when things were difficult gripped at my heart. I wrote a prayer to God. I prayed for strength. I prayed also for blessings to continue for my family and me and for us to remain close with one another. When finished, I tucked my requests to God inside my Prayer Capsule. I felt peace within knowing my prayer was in God's hands. I trusted He would answer according to what He knew was best.

Commit everything you do to the LORD.
Trust him, and he will help you. (Psalm 37:5 NLT)

I felt the reassurance of God that the experience of letting go of my daughter would build a stronger, happier, healthier bond between her and me. I prayed, then, for help in letting go, so God could do the work He promised and grow my relationship with Jenna even stronger than it was.

Jenna FaceTimed me that evening after getting all settled in with Lacy. She told me she loved me and encouraged me to use this time while she was away to finish my story that I had been working on for nearly ten years at that time. Seeing her smiling with her roommate and hearing an encouraging word lifted my spirits. I clung with hope to the promise God made about the relationship Jenna and I would be given. I wished Jenna a good rest of her evening and a good first day of school the following day.

It helped that school started for Dan and me the next day too. The workday was busy which helped to keep my mind off missing Jenna. She called and said she was overwhelmed, but doing well. Hearing her voice helped get me through the day. It seemed she was happy and that made me feel good.

On the weekends that Jenna came home, she and I enjoyed coffee dates, reminisced about old times, and shared like two girlfriends. Our relationship had already grown stronger within a short time of being apart from each other.

While at college, Jenna shared that she developed a desire to grow in her relationship with our Lord. I was pleased to hear that she wanted to read the Bible and start journaling like I had been doing. I gave her my Women's Bible with notes of my own written inside. I signed the Bible praying for Jenna to be encouraged and inspired by God's truth the way it inspired me and for her to grow in her walk with our Lord. After returning to her dorm, she sent me a picture, through a text message, of her Bible opened to the beginning with the caption, "Starting!"

I will give you a new heart and put a new
spirit within you. (Ezekiel 36:26 NKJV)

POINTS TO PONDER

Is shame interfering with your peace?

Are you struggling to let go of something dear to your heart or perhaps holding onto something that our Lord promises to replace with something even better?

It may seem like your world is falling apart, dear one, like you're losing what matters most to you, or like you've made too many mistakes for God to bless you. Our Lord has plans to prosper you though. God knows where you are and where you've been. Nothing is a surprise to Him. He knows where you are going and what doubts and fear, insecurity and feelings of unworthiness, shame, self-pity, and uncertainty you may cling to that hold you back from fulfilling His purpose in your life. He knows what it's going to take to get you where He wants you to be and what it will take for a calloused heart to soften toward His love, mercy, and grace to surrender, to trust, and to hope in Him. Believe, my friend, that God has a purpose for every experience and season in your life and that He wants to bless you! You may not understand at the time of a crisis, keep the faith, however, that God has a plan!

> *And without faith it is impossible to please him, for whoever would draw near to God must believe that he exists and that he rewards those who seek him. (Hebrews 11:6 ESV)*

Prayer: Thank You, Lord, that You know everything about me, what I've done, and where I've been and that You still love me. Thank You for giving me the strength to endure every circumstance that I experience. Forgive me, please, for the times I lose my focus and fall into the pit of sorrow. Help me, please, to surrender my heart to You, to believe in Your promises, and to be determined not to lose hope so You can do a mighty work in me and lead me to my calling even when my world looks bleak. Thank You that I am who You say I am rather than who others say I am. Thank You for Your blessings and that Your words are promises I can count on. I pray this in Your holy name, Jesus. Amen.

Chapter 19

RECEIVE

May he grant your heart's desires and make all your plans succeed.

—Psalm 20:4 (NLT)

At the end of Jenna's first semester and after much prayer and conversation between the two of us, Jenna made the decision to transfer to the local college in our community. As it turned out, Jenna experienced a "home-sick" feeling while away. Perhaps like me, when I left home, her heart longed more for what she left behind and less for what was out there.

After arriving home and starting her second semester with a degree in Business Marketing, Jenna began to connect with praise music and actually looked forward to attending church. I was confident that the Lord was working on her heart and believed that her experience away from home served a purpose. Because of it, she leaned on the Lord and opened her heart to Him.

> *Therefore if any man be in Christ, he is a new creature: old things are passed away; behold, all things have become new. (2 Corinthians 5:17 KJ21)*

I was thankful that the bond between Jenna and I grew stronger, happier, and healthier just like God promised it would! God knows what He is doing. He is a good God! My heart was happy to have my daughter back!

> *You will grieve, but your grief will suddenly*
> *turn to wonderful joy. (John 16:20b NLT)*

Jenna and I visited on a spiritual level and carried on conversations about God moments we experienced. She lifted my spirits by listening with an understanding heart and by offering words of wisdom and encouragement when I felt down from missing Eric and worrying that he and I would lose connection. Jenna encouraged me to look forward to what was to come such as grandchildren, possibly living back in the countryside, and living my dream to lead others to Jesus instead of dwelling on what I missed.

Jenna was right. I wasn't going to get anywhere wallowing in self-pity, wishing I had what I was used to. I believed God had spoken through her like He had done in the past. It was important that I praise God for all that He did and for the good that was on the way, for I'd never have grandchildren if my children didn't first grow up and build a family of their own. Jenna was an inspiration I could count on!

> *Be joyful in hope, patient in affliction, faithful*
> *in prayer. (Romans 12:12 NIV)*

Shortly after my conversation with Jenna about letting go of what was, we attended a worship service. During the service, the worship band sang a new song called "Do It Again" by Elevation Worship. Once again, it appeared that God used a song to speak a message to my heart. The lyrics expressed that God had come through before where there seemed to be no way, and He'll do it again. A feeling of peace came over me; I felt led to praise God during that moment and to believe that He won't fail me with my relationship with my son.

While encouraged, I reminded myself of the promise I believed God spoke within my spirit over fifteen years ago that He would bless me with the desires of my heart. My fear of losing connection with Eric was replaced with a feeling of hope as I recalled countless times in the past that I feared when there was no reason to fear because God came through for me. The song, "Do It Again," became my prayer, for I believed God would continue to come through again and again.

> *The LORD will fight for you; you need only to be still. (Exodus 14:14 NIV)*

When my birthday arrived, Eric and Lauren surprised me with a visit, a present, and a heartwarming card. I enjoyed the pleasant surprise. I desired hope to believe that visits would continue. I wanted to appreciate that Eric and Lauren were only an hour away.

> *May the God of hope fill you with all joy and peace as you trust in him, so that you may overflow with hope by the power of the Holy Spirit. (Romans 15:13 NIV)*

One month later, on Mother's Day, I was touched by a gift given by Eric. It was an angel with the words, "You're never too old to need your mom." My spirit lifted when I read the words printed on the angel. I believed my son's gift was a sign from God letting me know that He won't let me down. Eric and Lauren also gave me a miniature yellow rose bush. I planted it outside to thrive, which it did. I was reminded of my mom's yellow rose bush, the one that Jenna and her friend picked roses from for me after I prayed the Novena for true love. In my heart of hope, I believed the yellow roses were God's promise to bless me with a lasting and loving relationship with my son and daughter forever, just like the yellow roses previously given were His promise for a happy marriage. There's freedom in praying and in knowing that God is in control of all our circumstances!

> *May the LORD richly bless both you and your*
> *children. (Psalm 115:14 TBL)*

The more I gave God praise, the more appreciative I was of my blessings. I was fortunate that I still had my parents in their golden years and blessed to have opportunity to visit them and to pray for them the way I had been prayed for. Not knowing how much longer I'd have them in my life, it remained a priority of mine to spend generous amounts of time with them and to do for them what I was able.

Dan was kind to join me; what mattered to me, mattered to him. I recognized that when he insisted that he come along for the visits and help where needed. I saw it also when I asked what his dream was and he responded, "My dream is your dream." He showed his support through daily prayer and constant encouragement with an expectation of seeing my dreams come true. Dan was more than I imagined God would have blessed me with for a husband.

Perhaps you have a special someone you are thankful for that you can count on for support and encouragement.

> Sometimes, the best things in life are not
> things at all...but the people that make you feel
> loved and cared for. (Author Unknown)

Fast forward several years after I worried about losing what had mattered so much to me. God was good to continue to shower blessings over my life. My relationship with both of my children continued to grow. I celebrated the birth of Eric and Lauren's children. That's right! I became a grandma and I loved it! My granddaughter and grandson filled my heart with love, laughter, and adventure. My grandchildren and I developed a connection within our hearts which I hadn't expected. I was beyond grateful for this gift. Witnessing the love and care my son and his wife had for their children was indeed a gift as well. My grandchildren brought such joy into my life—I couldn't imagine life without them. I felt needed and appreciated as a grandma and still as a mom. I still had a purpose. I took the opportunity to make memories with my son and his family… I do to this day!

Praise God, who did not ignore my prayer or
hold back his love from me. (Psalm 66:20 NCV)

Not only had my son and his wife become proud parents to a baby girl and later a baby boy, Eric was assigned the management position at the company's location where he was employed and Lauren opened a daycare and was able to stay home to care for their children. God indeed provides!

Jenna took an interest in helping with cooking, baking, and shopping for groceries while attending college. I liked having her in the kitchen experimenting with new recipes. I was grateful for our heart-to-heart talks, for opportunities to enjoy activities together like tennis and bike riding while catching the sunset, and simply for her time. After graduating with a Bachelor of Science Degree in Marketing, she accepted a job with a company that was growing in our community. She made new friends and blossomed into a fine, Christian woman.

Dan and I celebrated our fourth wedding anniversary. I came to realize that the reason I encountered Michael was perhaps for me to draw nearer to our Lord which developed a passion in me to teach of His goodness, such as the mission priest prophesied, and to be blessed with the love that I found in Dan.

You are blessed because you believed that the
Lord would do what he said. (Luke 1:45 NLT)

We celebrated my dad's ninety-fourth birthday as well and looked forward to celebrating his and Mom's sixty-ninth wedding anniversary. God has been good to give above and beyond, more than I deserve... I am surely blessed!

> *Praise the LORD! Give thanks to the Lord, for he is good! His faithful love endures forever. (Psalm 106:1 NLT)*

In addition to those blessings, twenty years after having developed a passion to lead others to our Lord, God opened a door for an opportunity for me to do so. I got involved with the Stephen Ministry Program and Woman to Woman Mentoring through the church and began ministering, with Christ being the center, to women in need. I continued to grow in my faith by helping others find hope and security in our Lord through listening, praying, and sharing experiences that led me to put my trust, faith, and hope in God.

> *For God is working in you, giving you the desire and the power to do what pleases him. (Philippians 2:13 NLT)*

The experiences that drew me closer to our Lord weren't all enjoyable. Many of them were frustrating, painful, and challenging. I'm grateful, however, for it was those difficulties that drove me to turn to Jesus which grew my children and me stronger and wiser in our faith. I learned it is so that blessings truly do come from our trials, pain, and tears like it says in the song, "Blessings." The song that God used to encourage me when I was angry and didn't want to go through yet another storm after my second marriage.

Much like the rain that is produced from thunder and lightning to grow the crops, the storms I suffered produced the faith that grew me into who I am...someone I now see as worthy. Through the storms and experiences God allowed, I discovered God in a way I didn't know before. I developed a personal relationship with Him and grew to find rest in His love, in His power, and in His promises to provide. From my suffering and experiences came a story, a story of hope, inspiration, and determination.

> *But rejoice to the extent that you partake of Christ's sufferings, that when His glory is revealed, you may also be glad with exceeding joy. (1 Peter 4:13 NKJV)*

I pray that my story will infuse your heart to draw near to our Lord, to discover His amazing love, and to put your hope and trust in His promises that you can count on. It is my hope that you will be inspired to invite God into every circumstance in your life and that you praise Him in the storms you face. I pray you see your struggles turn to blessings and that you realize that the most valuable lesson of all when faced with any struggle is to put your security and trust completely in our Lord and surrender to His purpose for your life. Our Lord is an awesome God! Be blessed, my friend, by living the life you were created to live so you can be a blessing to others!

> *I will praise you forever, O God, for what you have done. I will trust in your good name in the presence of your faithful people. (Psalm 52:9 NLT)*

POINTS TO PONDER

Where are you today with the dreams God has placed in your heart?

Are you giving our Lord praise, inviting Him into your circumstance, willing to receive, and trusting that He will come through for you? Or are you living with worry and fear that He has forgotten you?

You may wonder, my friend, if God will hear your prayer and come through for you. Dear one, God hasn't forgotten you, nor the dreams He has placed in your heart and the promises He has made. He won't leave or forsake you. Nor will He give you a dream and then take it back. What He started, He will bring to completion, for

He is a God you can count on. He can take your brokenness, where you've been and the struggles you're facing to move you closer to His purpose for you. He will use it for His glory and He will bless you. Praise God then, in the storm without ceasing. Trust that He will take you down the road He knows you need to go to bring you a changed heart and awakened spirit. Believe in His power and promises. Be willing to receive His love, mercy, and grace and to accept the gifts He has for you—gifts you never imagined or thought were impossible.

> *Now unto him that is able to do exceedingly abundantly above all that we ask or think, according to the power that worketh in us. (Ephesians 3:20 KJB)*

Prayer: Heavenly Father, thank You that You are faithful. Forgive me, for the times I put limits on You that keep me from receiving the gifts You have in store for me and for the times I fail to believe You'll come through and make a way. Thank You for loving me no matter where I am in my walk with You. Help me to always worship and praise You no matter the circumstance. Help me to tune out the chatter and invite you into all my circumstances, to believe there's power in prayer, and to open my heart to receiving all that You want to give. Help me also to recognize what You have done for me and to give You the glory. I pray that my brokenness brings me to You and that Your love will bless me indeed and heal where healing is needed! Thank You for those who You have put into my life to support, encourage, and inspire me. Let my hope, my security, my trust, and my faith be in You and in Your power and strength alone, dear Lord, and let me rest in Your Holy Spirit's presence. I pray this in Your holy and precious name. Amen.

> *So do not throw away this confident trust in the Lord. Remember the great reward it brings you! (Hebrews 10:35 NLT)*

Are there desires in your heart and dreams you wish would come true—dreams that don't seem possible? Dear one, we serve a big and mighty God, a God that loves to give and that can make all things possible, even when it looks impossible. Stand on the promises of God to be faithful, for *Jeremiah 17:7 (NCV)* says, *"But the person who trusts in the LORD will be blessed."*

Our Lord will be faithful to come through for you, my friend! Trust and believe, *"And as you have believed, so let it be done for you" (Matthew 8:13 NKJV).*

About the Author

Sheila, Cofounder and Co-owner of the Prayer Capsule, is the mother of two, a son and a daughter, and the grandmother of two grandchildren as of now. She is the stepmother of two, a stepdaughter and a stepson and the wife to a husband whose dream is to see her dream come true. She is a Stephen Minister, Woman to Woman Mentor, two-time attendee of the Proverbs 31 She Speaks Conference, and a member of the John Maxwell Team certified to coach, teach, speak, and train. In the events of two failed marriages, she drew close to the Lord, which grew her faith in Him. She is passionate about helping others to seek our Lord in their times of need and to put their hope in His promises. It is her hope that her experiences will inspire others to believe there is power in prayer. She encourages others to put their trust in the Lord, to have faith in His loving care to provide for their needs, and to develop a relationship with Him through trials they may face. She is a child of our Heavenly Father, Who is all-knowing, all-powerful, and all-loving and the same yesterday, today, and tomorrow!

To learn more about the Prayer Capsule or to connect with Sheila, visit her website at sheilamalsam.com.